THE
HEART *of A*
DAD

A Faith Based Approach to Parenting

GEORGE GIBBS II

WESTBOW
PRESS®
A DIVISION OF THOMAS NELSON
& ZONDERVAN

THE HOLY BIBLE, NEW INTERNATIONAL VERSION®,
NIV® Copyright © 1973, 1978, 1984, 2011 by Biblica, Inc.®
Used by permission. All rights reserved worldwide.

Scripture taken from the New King James Version®. Copyright © 1982
by Thomas Nelson. Used by permission. All rights reserved.

Scripture taken from the NEW AMERICAN STANDARD BIBLE®,
Copyright © 1960, 1962, 1963, 1968, 1971, 1972, 1973, 1975, 1977,
1995 by The Lockman Foundation. Used by permission.

Scripture taken from the King James Version of the Bible.

WestBow Press books may be ordered through booksellers or by contacting:

WestBow Press
A Division of Thomas Nelson & Zondervan
1663 Liberty Drive
Bloomington, IN 47403
www.westbowpress.com
1 (866) 928-1240

ISBN: 978-1-9736-1377-0 (sc)
ISBN: 978-1-9736-1376-3 (hc)
ISBN: 978-1-9736-1378-7 (e)

Library of Congress Control Number: 2018900458

Print information available on the last page.

WestBow Press rev. date: 03/02/2018

TABLE OF CONTENTS

FOREWORD

The Man

I have known the author since his college days. I admired him back then as a young man, and now I have even more admiration for him.

George has successfully steered three ships or vessels to safe harbor during more than three decades, and through treacherous waters. Gibbs could easily be the envy of many for steering all three ships- his family, his corporate career, and his Christian ministry- each into safe harbor. Gibbs is a biblical husband and father, who has earned the loving admiration, and respect of his children. My congratulations to you George and Teresa, you have raised three beautiful young adults, of whom you have every reason to be proud.

After thirty years in Corporate America, Gibbs has accumulated the appropriate achievements to match his service years. Perhaps a precious few might not quickly trade places with him. Steering his commitment to Christian ministry might well be pivotal to the safe docking of his other two ships. To George, Christian ministry is about leading a Christian home; it is about ethical and godly practices in the marketplace. For one will find George Gibbs at the core is a godly man. He is a man seeking each day to honor his God, whether in his home, in his corporate offices, or in a pulpit. Each one of his vessels is open and available for public scrutiny.

The Book

Early in his book Rev. George Gibbs lays a foundation for framing his story, <u>The Heart of a Dad.</u>

First he asserts it and then proves the vital connection between his father/son relationship with his father; and his relationship as the father with his son. But the richness of Gibbs' story is even more heightened. He gives a glimpse into his African American, male, multigenerational rearing. Readers enjoy an insiders' view into how Gibbs' life was impacted by his relationships with his dad and both his grandfathers. This is indeed a beneficial, unique, wonderful and extraordinary backdrop for readers of his book.

Gibbs is an exceptional storyteller, no doubt helped along by his skills as a black preacher. But even the best storyteller needs a good story and there is no shortage of good stories in <u>The Heart of a Dad</u>. But the stories being told serve their proper purpose of giving light, opening wide the windows delivering one deep truth after another.

Gibbs is as effective host as he is storyteller. <u>The Heart of a Dad</u> is Rev. George Gibbs being transparent about those individuals and things near and dear to his heart. He will graciously introduce you to so many cherished individuals. No surprise that his Lord and the Scriptures pop up everywhere. Readers will hear meaningful edifying stories about his family as a whole and individually. His children return again and again. Then there are those who influenced George along his journey receiving their due. When the reader has finished the book one might reminisce from time to time about characters in the book. That is part of the strategy to help readers to reap the book's full benefit.

The passion of Gibbs the preacher can be heard in his pleas to fathers. He becomes an evangelist making the case why women need to get <u>The Heart of a Dad</u> into the hands of men they care about.

Churches are urged to rescue children suffering from absent dads by using The Heart of a Dad to build up a force of surrogate fathers.

After fifty years of ministry, most of those years spent developing leaders; I count myself a success if I had a hand in developing half a dozen like Rev. George Gibbs. And especially that part about being a biblical dad.

I am delighted to recommend, The Heart of a Dad, to the wide audience it deserves. May God favor as many men, families, and churches, as will read this book, and to the glory of God, apply what is being taught.

Dr. Willie O. Peterson
"Helping Christian Leaders to Ask the Right Questions"
Senior Executive Advisor
Coppell, Texas
2015

DEDICATION

This book is dedicated to the four most important people
in this world to me: my three children,
Courtney, Nathan and Tracey, and
their mother, Teresa, who has been on this uncharted journey with me
for 36 years of marriage. Thank you for your patience and support
of "The Heart of a Dad." Without your love
and support none of this would
have been possible and I want you to know three things:
I love you,
I support you,
I am on your side!

DEDICATION

ACKNOWLEDGEMENTS

First and foremost, I want to thank my wife, Teresa, who graciously allowed me to disturb her sleep morning after morning for over a year as I rolled out of bed between 2-4 a.m. and made my way into my study to write. Then, I want to thank those men who many years ago modeled faith-based parenting for a young father such as me. Men like my first two pastors: the late Bishop Odell McCollum, pastor of Gospel Tabernacle United Holy Church of America Inc., and my second pastor, Dr. Eddie B. Lane, pastor of Bibleway Bible Church of Dallas Texas. I also want to thank two men who challenged me to think not only practically but theologically about this subject; my good friend the Rev. Lafayette Holland, who specifically challenged me to think theologically, and Dr. Willie O. Peterson, who challenged me to explore the more practical dimensions and value of such a book.

Last, and independently, I want to acknowledge my dad, Harold Gibbs, who would have been 87 years old today. Unfortunately, he left us too soon, but he left an indelible imprint on my life. He was not only my dad and my friend, but he was my hero and, after more than 25 years, I still miss him and think of him every day of my life. It is because of what he instilled in me that "The Heart of a Dad" is a reality today. I know he is watching from a different vantage point and I hope and pray that my life has made him as proud as his life has made me.

INTRODUCTION

In the late 1980s when I was an area human resources representative responsible for staffing several facilities throughout North Texas it was engrained into our Human Resources Department that when we hired someone we were entering into a "psychological contract" with that new hire. There were built in and assumed expectations on both sides of that unwritten contract. Some of those expectations included things like being treated fair by the company; honesty and integrity was a built in expectation; a fair days work for a fair days pay was an expectation within that psychological contract. A safe work environment along with working safely was built into that contract. Punctuality and being paid as scheduled was built into that contract. There were many things that employees expected from the company and there were many things that the company expected from its newly hired employees which made up the psychological contract. While the contract was for the most part unwritten it was not unexpected. As dads, we, too, are in a psychological contract with our children. There are expectations on both sides.

"The Heart of a Dad" is really about how we fathers become dads to our children and how we live out the "Psychological Contract" with them. I argue that the burden of the relationship between father and child is on the father. It is not necessarily up to the children to ensure that they maintain a strong and vibrant relationship with their dad, but it is up to fathers to ensure that they cultivate their relationship with their children. I further argue that it is the dad's responsibility to lead his children in their development into adulthood using the wisdom of God. In addition to this unwritten contract, and of greater importance, is the spiritual obligation placed on a dad's heart that knits him together with his children for all eternity.

In "The Heart of a Dad," I not only provide a glimpse into my own upbringing and how the different relationships with my dad and grandfathers impacted my life, but I also share how I tried to use their impact on my life to impact the lives of our children. Nearly as important as the lessoned I learned from my fathers were the lessons that I learned from my spiritual mentors who also modeled for me what parenting from a faith-based approached looked like. However, where "The Heart of a Dad" separates itself from other how-to self-help books is in the fact that I extract lessons directly from the lives of true historical biblical characters. In many cases their lives were marked by failures as much as they were marked by successes. Either way, through success or through failure, I have tried to show that being a dad is a matter of the heart.

I conclude that in order for a father to become a dad he has to first cultivate his own relationship with his heavenly father through our Lord Jesus Christ. I argue that a dad's relationship with the Lord is what enables him to become the type of father that children call dad. However, the most important part of my argument is that the relationships that exist between God the Father and Jesus Christ His son is the preeminent model of what a father's relationship to his child or children should be. Between the Father and the Son there is a bond of fellowship and oneness that uniquely binds them together in ways that dads can and should seek to emulate. I argue that the nature of God the Father has inherent characteristics that provide a pattern for dads to follow to become godly in their character and their conduct toward their children.

Lastly, I challenge fathers to do better at becoming the dads that our children expect us to be. This means when sacrifice is required our children have an expectation that dad will make the sacrifice before he asks the children to make the sacrifice. When protection is required I argue that dads are the ones charged with providing protection for their families. However, the most important thing we dads can do is to become the spiritual shepherds of our families and be willing to do for them what the shepherds of Israel do for their sheep. They lay down their lives for their sheep. I challenge dads to demonstrate the type of love for our children that Christ demonstrated toward us in that he loved us unconditionally and, while we were yet at odds with him, He died for us.

PART ONE

Parenting through the Grid of Biblical Christianity

CHAPTER I

The Early Years

When my oldest daughter was preparing to go work on President Barack Obama's reelection campaign in Ohio, I told her that I would begin working on one of the books that was on my heart to write while she was gone. A couple months had passed over the summer of 2012 and I really had not done much writing. Although I talked with my daughter almost every day, while she was getting her job done, I was not getting done what I had promised her I would do. I borrowed my son's digital recorder that I bought some time ago to help him through his college course work to start recording "The Heart of a Dad."

I think it will be beneficial if I begin with the relationship that I had with my father and grandfathers. My father served 21 years as a military non-commissioned officer in the United States Air Force. He traveled quite a bit, although the family didn't travel with him. My dad was often gone for two and three months at a time for his military service. I looked forward to those times when dad came home, although they were a bittersweet pill; it was bitter when he had to leave for the next duty assignment and it was sweet when he would return. As a young boy, I always looked forward to dad coming home; he and I would oftentimes go into the basement of our family home in Columbus and we would build wood projects together. I remember that he and I worked on my first Cub Scout project in the basement. We built a log cabin out of wood dials in that basement. We also built a very unique coffee table that had six stools that slid under the table; it was a replica of a table that he no doubt saw during his travels around the world.

My dad loved to play chess; in fact, he was a pretty good player. When I was about eight or nine years old, he began teaching me how to play. He and I would sit in the front room of our family home and play chess for hours. We would sit in front of the picture window and just play game after game. Dad tried to teach my brother and sister, but they really didn't have much interest in learning the game beyond the basic direction in which the pieces moved. However, for me, it was about playing against my dad's mind. For me, it was about getting into my dad's mind and trying to understand how he thought. It was a thrill watching him think and act strategically. Oftentimes, I would make a move and he would tell me to take that move back because he knew I was not looking at the entire board and there were things that I was not seeing that would lead to a quick defeat. He was teaching me how to approach life with caution and from a strategic advantage.

My dad was not an easy man; in fact, he was often a hard man. My siblings and I grew up in an era in which parents did not believe in "time out." It was a matter of how much time it took dad to get up the stairs and get his belt off – that's the type of "time out" we received. My dad had high standards for us, he had big dreams and goals for us and he held us accountable, but he was also a fun dad. I can remember that dad would come outside in our back yard and play baseball with the kids from the neighborhood. Growing up, I thought our yard was huge, maybe because I had to cut the grass and rake the leaves, however, when I go back home now, I realize that our yard is really not that big after all. However, we were able to get four bases out of it: the corner of the garage was first base; midway in the yard was second, the fence post was third and home base was just next to the patio. From time to time, dad would race with us in the back alley; he wasn't much of an athlete, I guess I should say he wasn't much of a basketball player, but he did teach my brother and me how to box. He and my grandfather were both part of the Philadelphia boxing scene.

Once a month the family would climb into the family station wagon and go to the Air Force base to buy groceries. We would always count the bags of groceries; this would determine how many goodies we would have for the month. Dad would often take us to the bowling alley on the base and teach us the fine art of bowling. Growing up with my dad was really an enjoyable time. Unfortunately, those enjoyable times did not last into adolescence. My parents, like many other military families that had come through the Vietnam War Era, divorced when I was 12 years old. So when I think about my own heart as a dad, it really is wrapped up in the things that I learned and experienced with my dad while growing up. Even after the divorce, my dad was always around. He didn't stay away, but would oftentimes come around just to see his kids. We lived on a main a street that took you to the freeway so it was a busy street, but we played in the street every day. I remember when we'd play football in the street, I would always look to see what color car was coming around the corner. Was it that dark red Volkswagen station wagon? Later on, dad moved up as they say and he bought a silver and black Cadillac Sedan de Ville in the mid to late '70s; I would look for that Cadillac to turn the corner every day. You see, my dad coming by to see us said to my friends and neighbors that I, too, had a dad. In our neighborhood most of the fathers were still with their families, so when my dad came around he allowed us to feel as though we were equal to our friends. I had one friend in the neighborhood named David, whose dad wasn't around either, so he and I connected on that level, unlike the rest of the guys in the neighborhood. Everyone else had their fathers around which made life interesting for me growing up as a young man waiting to see my dad come around that corner.

One of the most important things that my dad did for me was to provide me with boundaries. Once he was gone the boundaries became even more pronounced; I realized then what he had really given me while he and my mother were married. Although the boundaries were in place, his absence left a void in the home without him there to strictly enforce them, so I simply stepped right over them. As a result, my youth became somewhat troubled, checkered and full of things of which I am neither proud or have any desire to rehash. One thing I did as a young teen was to work. Once dad left, it was not about working because you wanted to, but you worked because you had to work. I had my first job – a paper route – when I was 10 or 11 years old. Later on, I worked for a company called Jobs for Kids and traveled the state of Ohio selling candy door to door. After that, I worked for one of the premier steakhouses in the city of Columbus and later went on to work in a number of big warehouses throughout the city. After the divorce, I focused less on finishing school and more on working. If you wanted to have clothes and shoes and things like your friends had, you had to work. Although my dad paid child support for six kids, it was not that much. I wonder where we would have been had he not paid the child support. Although it wasn't that much and it decreased as each of us aged out, I am grateful that he paid what he did.

Dad never failed to let us know that he loved us. When we visited his place, we never left empty handed; he would always give us things to show his love. My dad gave me and my sisters and brother all kinds of things. I recall one day he gave me a video camera and then he gave me an old 35mm camera. When his life took another wrong turn, he gave all of his living room and dining room furniture to my brother. Before he passed away in 1990, he made sure that he gave my youngest sister money for her future wedding expenses. He made sure that all of his possessions went to his children. He made sure that we were a priority in his life and that we knew it. Each child was an individual and he made sure that we received his undivided attention; much like my Granddad would do the few opportunities we had to visit with him.

My Granddad George, for whom I am named, was the only blind boxing trainer at the time of his death. When he passed away the headlines read "George Gibbs, Blind Fight Trainer, Dies."[1] Granddad George, according to his obituary, trained fighters for 36 years, in spite of being blind. He lost his sight in 1935 after a bout with a fighter named Benny Bass. During his career, he fought many of the then lightweight fighters, including Bass, Tony Magilo, Johnny Jadick, Billy Wallace, Eddie Cool and Tony Falco.

Granddad George trained fighters using the sound method. The Philadelphia newspaper article said, "Gibbs, the world's only blind trainer, used the 'sound' method to get his fighters into shape. He would listen to their movements. When one of his pupils made the wrong move he would call a halt to the training session and tell his boxer what he was doing wrong and what steps to take in order to correct the error."[2] Veteran trainer and manager Joe Gramby told the paper "George is unbelievable." He said, "You can speak to him once and from then on he recognized you by the tone of your voice."[3] Reportedly, Granddad George's method of training a fighter was indescribable because of the way he was able to pick up on a fighter's movements and technique by merely listening to his footwork and the way he hit the bags – things many other trainers missed.

I never saw my granddad train a fighter, but I vividly recall him touching me and my siblings on our heads to determine who we were. I have always taken great pride in the fact that I was named after my grandfather, even though as a young child the name George was often the butt of many nursery rhymes. Pride in who I am has outweighed any teasing from my childhood. I knew my grandfather on my mother's side much better because he lived in Ohio with us for many years before he died. His name was William Hudson but we simply called him pop. Pop lived well into his eighties and he and my grandmother had 10 children. My grandfather retired from Budd's Industries in Philadelphia and my grandmother was what they called a domestic – she maintained the home of a Jewish family. Pop liked to walk; I suppose he liked to walk because I never knew him to drive a car. After my dad was stationed at Rickenbacker Air Force Base and my family moved from Philadelphia to Columbus, Ohio, my grandparents also moved to Columbus. The move from Philadelphia to Columbus was one of the best things to ever happen to our family. The move changed the trajectory of our family.

My grandparents restarted their lives well into their sixties and seventies. My grandparents were not the type to pursue higher education nor did they press us to do so. They simply worked hard and raised their family of 10 children. My granddad always talked about how he loved his children; he would call them each by name. My grandparents lived during the Great Depression; my parents were born in the 1930s, just after it started. Life was about working and surviving, not going off to college. My siblings and I were the first generation college graduates in our family. Our parents wanted to see us educated, but knew they could not afford to pay for us to attend college. When I left Columbus and moved to Dallas, Texas to attend Dallas Bible College my parents and grandparents were so proud, although they could not help with the cost of my education.

I came home after the first semester of college and told my dad I thought I wanted to get married, but I was concerned about the lack of financial resources necessary to make a marriage work. Dad shared with me one of the two pieces of marital advice that he ever gave me. He told me not to worry about money; money would take care of itself. At this point, I have to tell you that it has worked itself out. After 36 years of marriage, three homes, putting three kids in or through college and at least a dozen vehicles later, I can truly say that God has provided abundantly for my family.

The other piece of advice came three years later when dad moved to Texas to live with Teresa and I during his life's re-start. He told me that I did not need to say something about everything that my wife did or didn't do. My dad could give good advice, but he struggled with taking his own advice. When he came to live with us he was at the end of his fourth marriage. My mom called me the day before he arrived to let me know he was on his way and that I was to take care of him and she would explain later. When he arrived, I was a junior in college, working a part-time job and serving in the Texas National Guard, but I was charged with taking care of my dad. During this same time, Teresa and I were going through a difficult patch in our lives together. We were down to my two part-time incomes and things were not looking good at all.; It was during this time that dad shared his words of wisdom.

My dad was a very capable man. As a climate control engineer, he maintained the internal climate in museums and similar facilities. So he immediately went to work and began taking care of his business. However, those words that my mother had spoken to me – "take care of him" – constantly rang in my mind. So I did something I knew he would enjoy; I broke out the chess set and we played chess. Unfortunately, the time we spent playing chess, I should have been either sleeping or studying, but we played chess and ate ice cream. But we made it through and I graduated on the five-year plan. That was OK though because we did the right thing and I think Teresa and I were largely responsible for my dad's recovery after the demise of marriage number four. I said two, but my dad actually gave me three pieces of sound advice regarding marriage. The third, and probably most important, piece of advice was: "Son, before you start a thing, consider how it is going to end." I believe this advice has kept me from having a lot of problems after I carefully thought things through.

Now that I had finished college and dad was emotionally stable, the question was "What next?" Teresa and I were at a crossroad. Do I continue on to seminary and put myself in a position to compete with other seminary graduates or do I work full time? In college it was drilled into us that our ministry competition was the Dallas Seminary graduates who lived in the area. Teresa and I had been married for five years and we wanted to start a family, so I decided to work full time and serve as an associate in ministry. There were two other factors that made my decision relatively easy. One, I was tired from all the late nights burning the oil trying to get papers finished, learning the Greek and Hebrew languages and studying the works of theologians that I had never heard of before starting college. Secondly, we were broke and we knew we would have to pay for seminary the same way we paid for college, out of our pockets. After having a conversation with my pastor, Dr. Eddie B. Lane, we made our decision. The advice Pastor Lane gave me, which I kept close to my vest, was, "George, what you don't want to do is get 40 years old and not have the credentials that you will need for the rest of your life." He said I would run out of what I learned in Bible college. I didn't see how that could happen, but it can if you don't keep up your study habits. So 12 years and three kids later I went back to Dallas Seminary for two years to work on my master's degree.

During that 12-year period of starting a family, I began learning how to be a dad. The first thing Teresa and I did was to save our money and buy our first home. I can vividly remember one of my good friends giving me grief over the old 1977 Toyota Corolla I drove, especially since he had a BMW along with a Corvette. However, I would always tell him that my little Toyota sleeps in its own garage at night while his Beamer and Corvette slept on the street or in the apartment complex parking lot. I recall our first home going from being affordable to unaffordable in less than three months. When we bought the house in November 1986 it was brand new; it had never been occupied so the taxes were assessed to it as an unoccupied property. However, the day we moved in, it was assessed as an occupied property and the property taxes immediately increased as a result. Oh, by the way, our daughter Courtney was born a couple months later and we went down to one income again. These were not easy times for us; in fact, they were very difficult times. Let me be completely transparent and tell you that living off of one income was not part of the plan. I did not agree with my wife's decision to stay home, but Teresa stuck to her position that God had given her this child and it was her job to raise her and she was not going to turn her over to someone else to raise for her.

Now, let me tell you that there were two or three other women in our local church who were also pregnant around the same time as Teresa and they, too, decided they would stay home from work and raise their newborns. I also have to tell you that there were several brothers in the church who were not very happy. Times were really tough. A couple of years into this thing our son Nathan was born, bringing tremendous joy to our lives. A couple years later our third child, Tracey, was born. By the time Tracey came along I had accepted that this was the way it was going to be, so make the best of it. I decided if we were going to have only one income it had to be as high as possible. Therefore, I had to become the best at what I did so that I could make the most that I could – and get promoted. I worked extremely hard at becoming the best at what I did. I also decided I would no longer work two jobs. I said one man, one job. Plus, by time Tracey was born, I had mellowed some and I realized that I could no longer be angry over the decisions of the past. I needed to love my wife and children or else they lose out and I would also lose out. It was during these times that God kept us together in spite of the difficulties. I must confess that I was not just angry at my wife for not working and putting our lifestyle in jeopardy, but I was also angry at God for allowing it to be so, even though it was during this same time that God was teaching me how to trust Him. During these times Teresa and I never had too much, but we had everything that we needed and much that we desired to have. Although we were generous, sometimes to a fault, we never lacked anything. In fact, some of the best things that we have came during those times of leanness.

One of the things that I learned coming out of this lean period was that leanness doesn't last always. As the songwriter said: "Weeping may endure for the night, but joy comes in the morning." By the time we reached our 20th wedding anniversary God had blessed us with our second home in our neighborhood of choice. It was a five bedroom custom home on a corner lot with space for everyone including overnight guests. We bought the house from an elderly couple who had no intention of selling. I drove by the back of the house and saw a for sale sign in the garage, so I stopped and asked the owner if he was interested in selling the house and he said that he would consider selling it, but it was not on the market. The homeowner told me if we used a Realtor he would have to include the commission in the sale price, but if we didn't use a Realtor he could reduce the price. Immediately I said we didn't have to have a Realtor and within a week I went to the office supply store and got the papers to write up the contract and he and I entered into an agreement and we bought the house. The house was the perfect gift of God; in fact, it was the "flagship" home of the neighborhood. Moving to our second home was an opportunity for me to put my family in a better place, in a better school district, in a safer neighborhood.

We continued to live on just my salary. Unbeknown to me there were people watching how I managed to provide for my family with only one income. God was using our generosity to bless others and to bless Teresa and me, but He never told me this is what He was doing. It was at this time that I began to take inventory of my life and I realized I had been at it for so long and so hard that I really had not created any memories with our children. All of our neighbors took vacations and went to exciting places like the Bahamas and Disneyland, but we never took those types of vacations. The only vacations we took were trips to visit family in Ohio or Alabama. I decided we were going to start making memories of our own, so we began taking vacations and going places. However, the truth is I still could not rationalize spending the kind of money that my two-income family neighbors spent on vacations. But I have to admit that I was wrong, dead wrong! Our first real vacation was to Disney World in Orlando, Florida and to see the kids' faces light up as they did was worth every penny spent, and we spent a lot of pennies on that vacation. From that point on, I decided that as a dad it was my responsibility to create the memories if there were going to be any. So each year we tried to go somewhere special. We went to the Grand Canyon, Sea World, Phoenix, Arizona, New York City, and Washington, D.C. One year the kids and I went to St. Louis, Missouri and for 12 hours all we did was talk. I shared my entire life story with them. They were surprised to learn about the life their dad had lived. It was a long road trip, but it was worth every mile that we drove.

Lessons Learned from the Early Years:

1. Do what you promise.
2. Do something memorable with your children that will leave a positive, lasting impression upon them.
3. Dad's absence affects everything in a child's life.
4. Boundaries are established early in your children's development.
5. Dads instill pride and give meaning and purpose to their children.
6. Challenges in the early years prepare you for the latter-day obstacles.
7. Certain decisions made early on can prove to be life-altering turning points.
8. Be careful how you respond to decisions that you oppose; your response can do more damage than your opposition.
9. God uses our responses to difficulties to develop our testimony.

CHAPTER II

Raising Kids

In chapter one I talked about my relationship with my father and my relationship with my grandfathers and began to go into my relationship with my kids. I talked about the early years of raising a family on a single income and many of the challenges and blessings of living by faith and learning to trust the Lord.

In this chapter I want to take you back to what was the turning point for me in my life. I want to take you to the point where my life changed forever. When I was a 17-year-old high school senior, my life was changed forever. I became a Christian; I was "born again!" While growing up in Columbus, my best friend since second grade, Anthony, began talking to me about the Lord, and he invited me to attend church with his family. Seeing no harm in that, I went with them to Gospel Tabernacle Church, a Pentecostal Holiness Church, lead by Bishop Odell McCollum. Later that week, I was invited to a home Bible Study where the conviction of my heart seemed to be deepening within me. I was very unsure about what was happening to me, but I knew something was, and I knew I had to do something about what I was feeling. I couldn't wait to get to church the following week because I had decided to give my heart to the Lord. Now, for the record, let me say that Bishop McCollum was a gospel preaching pastor. By that, I mean every sermon was a gospel message that ended with an invitation to accept Christ into your life as your personal savior. In fact, Bishop McCollum sometimes gave the invitation before he reached the end of his sermon. When my sister gave her life to the Lord, she stood up while he was still preaching and said, "Preacher, I believe." However, for me it was a little different. During that second week, my heart was primed and ready to accept the Lord Jesus Christ as my savior at the end of the message; however, for the only time that I can remember in the four years that I would attend Gospel Tabernacle before moving away to Dallas, Bishop McCollum did not extend an invitation for people to accept Christ. I went the entire week terrified that I was going to die before getting back to church the following Sunday to give my life to Christ. At the time I did not know I could have given my life to Christ anywhere and it did not have to be in a church.

The week came to a close and I made it back to church for the third consecutive week and I was so ready to give my life to the Lord that I went to Bishop McCollum's office that morning prior to the start of service and introduced myself to him and told him that I wanted to give my life to the Lord. He replied, "Young man, that's good, but you will have an opportunity at the end of service today." Needless to say I don't remember a word of his sermon, but I do remember being nudged at the end of the message by my friend Anthony and my life has never been the same since that Sunday morning in March 1976 when I walked that 30 feet to the front of Gospel Tabernacle Church and gave my life to the Lord. Bishop McCollum knew I needed to take that walk from my seat to the front of the church; it was that public confession and profession of faith that, in his wisdom, he knew I needed. Had I simply stayed in his office, the congregation would only know what we told them happened; however, by me standing up and walking down front there were many witnesses to what happened in my life.

This act of faith was the turning point in my life and it has guided me throughout my life as a husband and father. As a result of that act of faith, being a father and dad was even more special to me because I wanted my kids to love me not only as their dad, but I also wanted them to love my Lord Jesus as well. The only way I could ensure that they would fall in love with Christ was that I had to be in love with the Lord. I believed they had to see that love manifested in the way that I love their mother; they had to see that love manifested in my service to the Lord and to others and they had to see that love manifested toward them. I have always told my kids three things: "I love you, I support you, and I am on your side." No matter what the situation, I always told them this, even when things were not going well. Another thing I always told them was: "There is a real devil in the world and he comes to do three things - steal, kill and destroy." We talked about what that means as far as the decisions they make every day of their lives. I wanted them to know that this enemy would kill their dreams, steal their aspirations, their hopes and their potential and destroy their futures, but in the midst of all that

> *Live life through the grid of biblical Christianity.*

I wanted them to know they have a dad who loves them, who supports them and who is always on their side.

My Christian faith has been the driving force in my life as I have tried to live within the biblical grid of Christianity. We certainly have not been perfect in this, but it's been our goal. Living this type of life means that sometimes I had to go against the grain, sometimes we had to stand alone in the deep waters of life and sometimes we didn't get to do what others did because it did not fit within our Christian lifestyle.

As the kids were growing up they began to get engaged with sports. Courtney started off playing basketball, but it really was not the sport for her so she put it down and began working within the church drama ministry. Nathan, on the other hand, picked up a basketball and has not put it down to this very day. He played a little football, but that really was not his sport; basketball became his love; if he could stay in the gym 24/7 he probably would. Tracey gravitated toward a number of sports; she started off playing soccer, then she picked up basketball, and, as she moved into middle school and high school, she began to play volleyball. So we spent a lot of time chasing balls around the southwestern portion of the country.

My wife and I spent a lot of time and money supporting our kids and other kids' dreams to play sports. We would go with the teams on road trips to games and on many occasions when it came time to eat half of the kids didn't have money so we bought breakfast, lunch or dinner. After a while, I began carrying my grill and we would fix hot dogs and hamburgers for the kids as a way to reduce costs. Although this was an expensive time for us, we had some of our greatest moments of joy and satisfaction during this season of our life as we watched our kids and other kids begin to grow and develop into young men and young ladies. Your kids can give you some of the highest highs, but they can also give you some of the lowest of lows.

Our kids have given us some of the greatest moments of joy in our life. For example, to see one of our daughters who struggled with math pass that math class and to see our son who put basketball above everything else begin to excel in the classroom brought great joy. To see our son overcome what people call disabilities and turn them into abilities brought us great joy. On several occasions, people have come up to me and said, "Brother Gibbs, I saw your son the other day, he didn't see me, but he was being such a gentleman by holding a door for an elderly lady." On more than one occasion, Teresa and I have had coaches thank us for how we raised our son. Although you hope your children behave as you've taught them, when they leave the house you really don't know what they are doing until you get these unsolicited reports. It's these unsolicited affirmations that brought great joy to our lives. When the algebra tutor says your daughter is getting it and you see her overcome her anxiety and go from underperforming to excelling – great joy. When your kids tell you what they want to be and do in life and it's something that will help society – great joy.

Just as our kids can bring us great joy they can also bring us some of the deepest sorrows. It's disheartening when you get a phone call from someone telling you that your child has done something that is wrong and does not meet the expectations that you set for them or you get a knock at the door and you open it and someone is standing there with an accusation against one of your children. It's in these moments that you begin to question yourself and your parenting skills. You ask yourself how could it be that your kids didn't get this?

Let me share with you a story about one of the things that brought us repeated moments of disappointment - tattoos. I am pretty certain that when God created us He put on us everything that we needed to be beautiful. The Bible says that we are fearfully and wonderfully made. So I have a strong aversion to getting tattoos.

My oldest daughter, who had graduated from high school, was walking around the house talking about colleges she was looking into and how she was preparing to go off to school in the fall. Out of the blue, she says she has something to show me and she raises her sweat pants leg up and shows me her tattoo. I was so disappointed because I thought for sure that we had that conversation and the kids knew full well how we felt. I began to think of how it could hinder her in the future and I began to wonder what does the Scripture say about this, because, again, I want to live within the biblical grid of Christianity. Not long after that, our son came in and I noticed something on his arm. Now I am not only disappointed, but I am angry because he can't say he didn't know how we felt; he knew and did it anyway. So we discussed tattoos as a family and our position was and is today that God provided us with everything we need on our bodies and it does not please Him when we go and ink them up with tattoos; besides all of the potential societal ramifications. After all of this discussion and sharing the Scriptures and knowing our personal viewpoint, our third child did the same thing. I was in the middle of a job relocation and I flew home one weekend only to discover that the youngest child had followed in her siblings' footsteps. At this point it was no longer about tattoos, it was about respect and the fact that all three of our kids had disrespected our wishes, our beliefs and the standards that we set for them. This was a difficult thing for me to get over, but I had to let it go. A friend of ours had gotten a tattoo on her leg – a small rose or butterfly – and when I saw it for the first time, although I am sure she thought it was attractive, I asked her why did she go and ruin a perfect set of legs? So with the kids, I reminded them of what I always said: there is a real devil in the world and he came to do three things – steal, kill and destroy.

Although disappointed, I also had to remind them that even though I did not approve of what they had done, I still loved them, I still supported them, and I was still on their side. Recently, Nathan and I were doing some research on international basketball clubs and in one of the club's information it said: "men with excessive tattoos need not apply." I found that to be very interesting. These young men may be the best basketball players around, but their decision to ink up their bodies could become the destroyer of their dreams to play professional basketball. Our kids have to know that there are things that can derail their dreams if not managed well in their youth.

Lessons Learned from Raising Kids:

1. One act of faith can change the trajectory of one's life.
2. Raising kids by faith means giving them space to grow, engage and experience new challenges.
3. Parenting by faith will provide you with unexpected moments of joy and unwanted disappointments.
4. Today's decision can become tomorrow's derailer.
5. Disappointments don't have to lead to dysfunction or destruction of the parent-child relationship when properly handled.

CHAPTER III

Supporting Your Kids' Dreams

I ended chapter two talking about kids and their dreams, and I said that some of the decisions our kids make can destroy their dreams before they have a chance to take root and began to grow and flourish into something special. One of the most important things we can do as dads when it comes to our kids and the dreams they have for themselves is to make sure that they know we are on their side. We have to take great care to ensure that we don't crush or belittle their dreams and aspirations. There is a delicate balance between supporting their dreams and helping them see that maybe a particular dream they have is not something that is realistic for them. This has been an ongoing process for my wife and I as we endeavored to support kids in their dreams. Our children have their own specific dreams and aspirations for their individual lives and, as dad, my responsibility is to support them. So the question becomes how do I support each child in his or her specific dream. When everyone is telling them what they can't accomplish and what they can't do and what they will never be, as dad, I have to be the one to remind them that with God all things are possible. This happens to be an area in which my wife and I are on separate sides of the same sheet of music. My wife, while she joins me in supporting our kids' dreams, tends to lean toward what she perceives as a more realistic approach. I, on the other hand, have a tendency to tell them what is possible. I think in terms of possibilities because, in my 40 years of walking with the Lord and depending on Him for my very existence and learning to trust Him in all my ways, I have seen and witnessed

God do what people said was impossible over and over again. So I challenge our kids to visualize what's possible.

As dad, I try to encourage my kids on a regular basis to follow their dreams and to never give up on them. I dream a lot, in fact, I would say I probably dream every day in the natural sense, and one of the things I realize about my dreams is they are most often dreams that occur in a context. By that, I mean I rarely dream about things that I have not been thinking about for some time. I don't know about you, but sometimes my dreams are as clear as day and I remember them when I wake up, but at other times there are those dreams that escape my memory in the morning. This lets me know that when it comes to our kids, not every dream they have will become a reality; some of their dreams are like my dreams that escape my memory because they are not in context. The other thing I observed about our kids and their dreams is that each child's dreams just like my dreams are individual and personal to them. Just like you can't have my dreams and I can't have your dreams, neither can your kids have one another's dreams. Dads and moms, you can't have or live your kids' dreams; they have to have their own dreams. Our role is to support their dreams.

Now faith is the substance of things hoped for, the evidence of things not seen.

So let me talk about why I can support dreams that are yet unborn. How is it that I can say that I have learned to trust God in the impossible? I told you in chapter one that my parents divorced when I was 12 years old. That was a turning point in my life and not necessarily for the better – I became quite a rebellious teenager. When dad left, life changed; for the first time that I can recall our mom had to go to work outside of the home. When you have six kids to support, court ordered child support just doesn't cut it. Mom often worked two jobs to ensure that the family had what we needed and I emphasize needed, not what we wanted. The truth of the matter is if you were old enough to work you went to work; myself along with my three older siblings all went to work doing something. I had so many jobs as a teenager, I am not sure I can remember them all. I sold candy door to door for Jobs for Kids; I worked in the summer jobs program cleaning the elementary school and getting it ready for the fall semester; I worked in a luggage store for a short period; my brother and I worked at a gas station where we had to keep the restrooms clean; and I told you earlier that I worked at one of the finest steakhouses in Columbus, Ohio. I have received a W-2 since I was 14 years old.

Working so much at a young age did a few things for me. One, it gave me a degree of freedom that I otherwise would not and maybe should not have had. Secondly, it provided me with experiences early in life that most kids my age did not have. Thirdly, and most detrimental, it distracted me from doing what most kids my age were doing, which was ensuring that my academic requirements were being appropriately satisfied. When I entered my senior year of high school, I was so far behind and needed so many credit hours to graduate that getting out of school that year seemed like it would be impossible. "But God!" I told you in chapter two that I became a Christian when I was 17; that was my senior year in high school. I started the year off needing 13 credit hours to graduate. My master plan was to transfer from my school district to attend school in the district where my dad lived. Although that was my master plan, it was not God's master plan, and it failed miserably. I transferred from South High School to Walnut Ridge High School at the start of my senior year, but soon realized I was too far behind and had inadequate study skills. I was not going to make it at that suburban high school. Within six weeks I transferred back to my old school and I began attending Central Adult High School in the evenings. I combined day and evening classes and took two classes in the summer, attended night school in the fall and graduated that year.

> *I can do all things through Christ who strengthens me.*

What does this have to do with supporting kids' dreams? Well, I dreamed of graduating from high school and going to college and having a successful life, but it didn't start off looking like that dream was going to become a reality. However, after I became a Christian mid-year of my senior year, God immediately began demonstrating His ability to provide for me and to work absolute miracles in my life. One of the first things God did was show me that He could keep me from stumbling and falling back into a life that I was trying to leave behind. I grew up in an era when families had five to six kids, unlike today when families average 2.5 kids. Growing up in this environment with dad gone, mom having to work, and working myself, meant I had resources to get me into things that were not always in my best interest. So when I became a Christian, I told the Lord, "If You can keep me from doing the things that I did before I accepted You, I will trust You the rest of my life." Well, here I am 40 years later still trusting Him.

After finishing high school, I had to figure out what I was going to do next and how to pay for it. I decided to go to college, but how do I pay for it? As I contemplated that question, I saw a TV commercial for the Ohio Army National Guard that said if you commit to six years of military service one weekend a month and two weeks in the summer the military would pay for your college education. I thought that's a no-brainer so I joined the Ohio Army National Guard. Little did I know, but it was through that experience that God would demonstrate His ability to me in a mighty and demonstrative way. There I was a kid fresh off the block, as they say, getting off the bus at Fort Knox in Louisville, Kentucky, home of the United States Bullion Depository, one of the most, if not the most, fortified military installations in the world. I felt like I had just entered a new dimension of life.

The first way God demonstrated what He was capable of was to have me – the kid from the block who was not supposed to make it – appointed the platoon leader. This meant I had to be out front at all times. Little did I realize at the time, but being out front all the time meant you always had people watching you; secondly, you always had people following you; and third, it meant that although you didn't have to be the fastest runner you had to become the strongest runner. You had to become the strongest runner because, as the platoon leader, you had to carry the Guidon, that is, the American flag. You may think that's not a big deal; well, maybe not until you have carried it for five miles running up and down the hills and mountains of Fort Knox in full battle gear. God showed me He could strengthen me, He could keep me, and He could exalt me. He also showed me I would no longer be seen as the kid who was not supposed to make it; the kid who was suspended no less than eight times in one school year; the kid who, as a ninth grader, was one of 12 guys who went through one of the first "Scared Straight" programs at the Mansfield Ohio Maximum Security State Penitentiary. Our school counselor, Mr. Buette, said we were the 12 students most likely to end up there. Instead, God showed me he would make me a leader among men. This is why I support my kids in their dreams.

When I finished basic training I was sent to Fort Benjamin Harris in Indianapolis, Indiana for another 13 weeks of school, where I studied journalism. I never imagined that years later I would become an author, but if you are reading this book, I have become more than I ever dreamed. I support my kids' dreams because I have seen God do the impossible; I have seen the last become the first; I have seen the hungry become full; I have seen the poor become rich; and I have seen the troubled be at peace. When I finished my military training and my Military Occupation Service training I returned to Columbus and went to work at WTVN-TV Channel 6. I started off as a floor director, the person who points the on air talent to the camera. I soon learned how to direct the men and women who operated the cameras and engineering equipment. I later directed public service shows and commercials and finally made it to occasionally direct the weekend news broadcast.

If only the story ended there, but it didn't – a young lady I attended elementary school with became an intern at WTVN. She was a senior in college and I was a freshman, but we were the same age, and, by the way, my job was to train her to do my job. I asked myself, "What's wrong with this picture?" I started to give serious consideration to where I was in life in respect to where I wanted to be, where my dreams were taking me and how would I get there. I decided I wanted something that would be lasting and eternal as compared to something that was temporal and short lived. I decided to leave Ohio State University, where my college tuition and books were being paid in full by the military, and move across the country to attend Dallas Bible College, a small little-known Bible college where I had to pay for everything myself. You're probably thinking that makes no sense and I would agree with you, unless that is God's plan for you, then it makes all the sense in the world.

Let me share with you why it makes sense. I left Columbus for Dallas in summer 1980 during a Texas heat wave. It had been 100 degrees or higher for more than 90 consecutive days. I boarded a Greyhound bus with a letter accepting me in school, a letter of recommendation and $400, which came from my last paycheck from the TV station. The bus made a stop in Broken Arrow, Oklahoma and I realized my sister and brother-in-law lived there, so I called them and told them what I was doing. I told them we had some down time before continuing on to Dallas and they came and got me and we went back to their house. My brother-in-law had a truck that he wanted to get rid of and he offered it to me for about $10 a week. I bought that old truck and headed to Dallas. When I arrived in Dallas, the first thing that caught my attention and got me jazzed up was twin gold-colored glass high-rise buildings. I thought this is a long way from Kelton. I had a friend, Larry Freeman, who was working on a master's degree in theology at Dallas Theological Seminary. Larry told me that when I got to Dallas I could room with him; little did I know he was rooming with someone and he really didn't have a place to stay. However, God was at work behind the scene. One thing I often tell my wife and kids is that God is always working behind the scene. When I got to town, Larry introduced me to another minister, Jim Carrington, who was about to graduate from Dallas Seminary. Jim told us we could stay at his place, but he only had one bed. Actually, he only had one room and a bathroom, so Larry and I slept on the floor.

I realized three things pretty quick: first, my $400 was not going to last long, especially trying to keep gas in that big truck. Second, I needed to find a job quick and third, I needed to get off of that floor. Within two weeks of arriving in Dallas I got hired on at UPS and I also got a job at Osborne Furniture Store and I started school. Soon after, Larry and I found an apartment and we moved in that day. My first furniture delivery was a new bedroom set to a lady and I asked her what she wanted us to do with the old mattresses and she said she didn't care, just get them out of there. I drove those mattresses straight to our apartment; no more sleeping on the floor. The owner of the furniture store sold me a few more pieces of furniture and we were in good shape. We had transportation, we had a place to live, we had a job so we could eat and pay rent and tuition – life was great; God had provided!

About a month later, a neighbor from across the hall came over one evening and said his car had cut off on his wife and she was stuck at a friend's house. He asked me if I would take him over there to see if we could get the car started. I said yes, of course. When we got there and his wife's friend stuck her head out the door, I asked myself "Who is that?" Now, let me say this, the last thing I wanted to do was to start dating someone, anyone. I was in Dallas to go to school and get my college degree. Well, three months later the friend who stuck her head out the door and I got engaged and seven months later we were married. Thirty six years and three kids later, we are still standing. I have seen God provide time and time again so supporting my kids as they pursue their dreams is easy. Because I have seen what God can and will do, I believe in what is possible. It's like going to the theater and seeing a live show being performed on stage or like when I worked at the TV station. What you see on stage or on the screen is only one part of the production;

you don't see everything that goes on behind the scene to make it an amazing show. God is like the producer/director and engineer working behind the scene, so it's easy for me to tell my kids with full assurance that God is working it out. I say go and watch God be God. I can share story after story when I had to go and watch God be God. I graduated college with multiple awards - the kid from the block. God has an amazing show planned for your kids' lives, but we dads have to let them dream and then support their dreams. The Scripture says... "No eye has seen, no ear has heard, no mind has conceived what God has prepared for those who love him." NIV (1 Corinthians 2:9)[4] There are times when God is opening doors miles away that we have no idea of; there are times when God is managing circumstances of which we have no idea, but it is necessary so that when we get to where he needs us to be everything has been made ready for us.

I recall being in Dallas on what we call a special assignment, my career was not moving as fast as I would have liked and I told my operations manager that if I didn't have a permanent assignment by a certain date it would become problematic. What I had to remind myself of was the fact that God was working behind the scene. Sometimes people are being used as instruments of the Lord and they don't even realize it. Before I relocated to California, I was in a little town called Greenwood, Mississippi on an audit when I got a call from my manager asking me if I was still interested in advancing my career. I asked myself what kind of question is that, but I told him of course I was. He told me to check with my family because there may be an opportunity available. He called me back the next day and told me to schedule a flight to Orange County, California to interview for a new assignment. Little did I know, but God was working behind the scene; a lot of pieces had to fall into place for the door of opportunity to open up for me to be slated to move to a place that is three time more expensive than Dallas. We lived in a beautiful five bedroom custom home in Dallas and when I told my wife that a home in Orange County would cost us more than three times as much as our Dallas home, you would have thought that I said the rapture came and we missed it. Her question was and years later still is: How can this be and how did we do that? My answer then was the same as it is now; God will provide, he has and he will continue to do so.

This reminds me of the story of Abraham and his son Isaac in which God told Abraham to go up to Mount Moriah where he was to sacrifice his son, but at the very last second God instructed Abraham to stay his hand. Then God said, "...Now I know that you fear God, because you have not withheld from me your son, your only son." NIV (Genesis 22:12) The place where God told Abraham to go was called Mount Moriah which means the place where God provides. I take it that when God leads us and directs us to go somewhere, anywhere, it becomes our "Mount Moriah," the place where God provides. So, for me, no matter how bleak things may look at the present time, it is the place where God will provide. If dads around the world would grab hold of this truth, supporting our kids as they pursue their dreams becomes an easy thing to do.

The Place Where God Provides

We have to be careful not to let what we perceive as achievable stifle our kids' dreams. Our oldest daughter was tall for her age when she was in the elementary school and she tried out for basketball and made the team, but it really wasn't her forte so she switched to drama and we discovered that she was pretty talented. Sometimes you have to let your kids explore their dreams to see what fits. Years later, my daughter told me she wanted to go to Clark Atlanta University. I asked, "What's a Clark Atlanta University and what's it going to cost?" Today she has a bachelor's degree from Clark and a master's degree from California State University, Long Beach. Where God leads, He provides. My son had dreams of playing basketball at the college level and winning a championship. The facts are he did play college basketball and he did win a state title, but we had to move to California for that dream to be realized. I saw my son's commitment to his dream and I realized that if he was that committed then certainly I could support him.

Oftentimes families emancipate their kids when they turn 18. Parents wipe their hands, say they have done their part and put their kids out. I say to parents don't wipe your hands so soon, your part's not finished. Growing up in our family, when my brother and sisters and I turned 18 we had six months and we had to go to college, the military, or somewhere. I said I would not do that to my kids even though there were times when I may have wanted to give up on their dreams. The truth is there were times particularly with our son that I said we had to get this boy out of here; he wants to be a man and we can't both be men in my house. In fact, there was a time when I did put him out, but quickly had a change of heart. I realized that if I gave up on him no one would take him in other than the criminal justice system and if he got caught up in it he would never reach his full potential. So, I went and got him and said come home. I told him we would work out the differences and learn to co-exist as he learns to become a man.

> Be still and know that I am God.

Our youngest daughter tried a number of things: soccer, basketball, volleyball, dance, and we supported her in all of those efforts. We have had enough musical instruments in our house to form a full band – clarinets, drums, trombone, saxophone, piano – and today nobody plays any of them, but we supported their dreams. Today our youngest is in college and doing well; not only are we supporting her dreams, but her dreams have become our dreams for her.

Let me close this chapter with another illustration of God performing the miraculous in our life. I told you that I worked at WTVN when I finished my basic training for the Ohio National Guard. Because I started out part time, I didn't make a lot of money, but I needed an affordable place to live. Wouldn't you know it, there were some affordable apartments within walking distance. They were what we called "the projects," a place where cities house their poor and low-income families. I got one of those low-income units for $5 a month, which was about all I could afford at the time. Later on I discovered that the senior citizen apartments directly across the street from the TV station had eight units that could be rented to non-seniors. I applied and I got a unit for $20 a month for an entire year. They were very nice carpeted one bedroom efficiencies.

While I was living there I got the opportunity to accompany my Army captain on a four-day trip to Minneapolis, Minnesota for a conference he was attending. Basically, I was the enlisted man who carried his bags and ran his errands for four days. When he came to pick me up at my apartment, I had just put a pot of water on the stove to fix a cup of tea. I was so nervous about taking the trip with my captain that I forgot to take the pot of water off the stove. Four days later when I returned home that pot set burning on my stove. The pot, though seared and vibrating on the stove top, had not caught fire, it had not cracked or exploded; it just set there vibrating on the burner. To this day I still have that pot. I don't think I'll ever get rid of it. God does miraculous things! That's why I can tell my kids: You trust God and you watch God. The Bible says, "Be still and know that I am God…" NIV (Psalm 46:10) "But they that wait upon the Lord will renew their strength; they shall mount up with wings as eagles, they shall run and not be weary, they shall walk and not faint." NIV (Isaiah 40:31) That's the message I've tried to instill in our kids. While I support their dreams, they need to have a faith of their own based on their experience with God.

When my kids had the choice to do something wrong or bad in order to get something good, I always told them we were not going to do that. Some parents in our community would occasionally have their kids mis-represent where they lived so they could attend what was perceived as a better school, but I told my kids we would not. I realized if I let my kids tell falsehoods to get them in a better place, then I was the liar and I'd be sending the message that if you wanted to get something better it was OK to be dishonest to get it.

I tried to demonstrate through my faith in God that whatever we needed God could and would provide and we did not have to try to game the system to get what we wanted or needed. As a result, some of our kids' dreams have been costly to support, but I would not change one thing.

Lessons Learned from Supporting Our Kids' Dreams:

1. Become your child's greatest cheerleader.
2. You can't relive your dreams through your kids.
3. With God all things are possible.
4. God can keep your kids focused and allow them to fulfill their dreams.
5. God will exalt you in due season if you allow him to order your steps.
6. While your kids may have dreams for their future; God has plans for their future.
7. God is always working on the plan behind the scene.
8. Life is not lived by coincidence or luck; the steps of the righteous are ordered even when we don't see or know the order.
9. Supporting your kids' dreams will always take you to Mount Moriah – the place where God provides.
10. Dreams take time to develop into reality and sometimes we have to be still and wait for God's perfect timing.

Theresa Bridget Photography

CHAPTER IV

Uncharted Waters

Yesterday (Oct. 8, 2014) my dad would have celebrated his 84th birthday, had he lived to see it. When I arrived in my office yesterday I began to think about what life might have been like if my dad had been with us for these last 22 years. Had dad been here he would have watched his grandson and granddaughters grow into the young man and young women that they have become. The last photo we took of my dad was of him holding Courtney and Nathan on his lap. Courtney was two and a half years old and Nathan was just about six months old. At the time of the picture dad was already stricken with cancer, which would take his life just a few days later. I suspect life would have been very interesting had he been a part of their growing years.

Regretfully, my kids, like I did, will have some uncharted waters in their life. They will never be able to say that they knew their granddad and had the opportunity to bond with him and learn from him. I suspect he would have done the things with them that he did with us and he would have been as generous with them as he was with me and my brother and sisters. I regret that my kids didn't get to spend time with their granddad and learn from his travels around the world. He had a 9 foot by 12 foot wall map of the world that had push pins in it to represent all the places he had traveled to during his military service. He was a decorated soldier in both the Korean Conflict and the Vietnam War. He traveled to Japan, China, Peru, Panama, France, Germany, Italy and Whales, just to mention a few places to which he traveled. I would venture to say that anywhere there was an Air Force base in the United States, he had been at least once. He gained so much knowledge that he was like a walking National Geographic magazine. The kids would have learned so much from him.

The uncharted waters that I want to share with you are those years that I did not get to spend with my dad and how those years impacted the same period of time in my kids' lives. Mom and dad divorced when I was 12 and dad left, so I did not have a father role model in my life or an example of what a dad should do. In turn, when it came to dating process and evaluating who and when our children should date, I had no model. There was that period of time when I missed the wise counsel that I should have gotten. I didn't learn from my dad how to navigate through the difficult years of marriage and child rearing. There was not a model to pattern my fatherhood after so I decided I would use the biblical model. So I had to know what that model looked like and how that model played itself out practically.

The biblical model for me started with "Fathers, do not provoke your children to anger." So I spent a lot of time talking through situations with our kids, maybe to a fault. There may have been times when I should have put my foot down and just said this is the way it's going to be because I said so. However, oftentimes I talked more than I should have. The other thing I did was to look at the lives of biblical characters like the patriarch Jacob and Israel's King David to see how they managed being a dad to see what I could learn from them. One thing they both did that had devastating effects on their families was they had favorites. In both cases the results were murderous. You recall the story of Jacob and his favorite son Joseph, whose brothers resented him because his father loved him more. So I have done my level best not to have favorites among my children.

I love my three children equally, but separately. Each one of our children is different, therefore, our love for them, though equally felt, is different. I love Courtney, our first born, in ways that you could never imagine. When she was born, she was the apple of my eye and growing up she was a phenomenal young lady. I love her with all my heart. My youngest daughter Tracey was also the apple of my eye, but in contrast to her sister, she was more of a daddy's girl. Courtney and I would rub noses; Tracey and I would hug. Tracey is independent minded. I love her equally with all of my heart. Courtney and Tracey have totally different personalities, but I love them both the same. Our son Nathan, on the other hand, is obviously different from his two sisters, but it doesn't mean we love him any less, just different. The girls would often accuse my wife and I of treating Nathan differently, and they are right. We do treat him differently because he is a young man. When he was a boy I treated him like someone who would one day become a young man and when he became a young man I began treating him like someone who would soon become a man. Once when Tracey accused us of treating her brother differently, I explained to her that she could not do the same things he did and still be called a lady. She accused us of playing favorites by allowing Nathan to have liberties that she did not have. There were multiple reasons why he had liberties that she did not have. First, he was older. Secondly, as a young man there were some things I knew he had to get out of his system and trying to hold him back could prove more detrimental to his development into manhood. Thirdly, I decided, particularly with my son, to pick my battles wisely; to major on the majors and minor on the minors.

A couple of years ago I attended a United Way luncheon at an automotive museum to kick off the organization's annual fundraising campaign. Inside the museum were no less than 40 amazing mostly European classic luxury vehicles; everything from sports cars to high-end luxury sedans. The owner was there and he took the time to share with us some of the nuances about the cars and what made each one special. A man asked the owner which car was his favorite to drive if he could only pick one. The owner responded with his own question and asked the man, "Do you have kids?" The man said he had three daughters. The owner asked, "Which one is your favorite?" The man nodded his head without speaking, because there is no answer other than "they all are." To my dad, I am confident that we all were his favorite just like all three of our kids are my favorite.

As I entered the period of uncharted waters in the lives of my children I tried to identify what each child needed and how their individual differences required different responses from me. One needed shoes while the other needed a coat and the other one needed a hat, they each had different needs. Their physical needs were much easier to meet, but a lot of the time I was in uncharted waters in certain areas of their development. Because my father was no longer there for me to turn to, I found other models that I could learn from. I looked at some of my colleagues at work and in ministry to see how they did things; some of which I could emulate and some I could not. For example, one colleague told me he spent a considerable amount of money on college exam preparation for his kids. While I was unable to spend the kind of money that he spent, I learned that preparation for the standardized college exams was important; now the question was how to get it done within our means. My pastor, Dr. Lane, provided me with several demonstrations of how to be a dad in these uncharted waters. As his kids became teenagers, like most kids, they wanted to get after school jobs, but he didn't allow them to until they were older. You see, he realized the money they would make at some fast food joint would not make up for what they would miss academically.

Breadth of Perspective Leads to Opportunity

I once asked Dr. Lane when was he going to write his first book; everyone else seemed to be writing books and I knew he was just as qualified, if not more so, than the guys who were cranking out book after book. My question was what was he waiting on. All these other preachers were putting out less than scholarly materials, why was he not offering the public the benefit of his 30 plus years of ministry and academic experience. His answer was short yet profound. He said, "I'm raising my family; there will be time for that." Today, if you Google him you will see he has published at least eight books. He was saying that his children meant more to him than the praise of men. You can do great things and receive the praise of men and lose the most important things in your life. I can't begin to tell you how many of my colleagues at work and in ministry gain fortune and fame, but lose the best part of life in the process.

Some of the things I learned from my friends, colleagues and ministry partners were what not to do. Many of them used to work multiple jobs. Now if you have to work more than one job to provide for your family, do so. However, I decided early on that I would no longer work several jobs. I realized I had to have energy for my family and working more than one would drain me of the necessary energy to be a dad. One of the things I discovered was when dads are not home, particularly at night, because they are working night shifts or holding down another job, things happen in their absence. When dad is not in the home other men, young and old, will come around and act like they are running things. I can vividly recall while visiting my in-laws on one of those going home vacations I was in the bedroom lying down and the family was out in the den, except my father-in-law, who was at work, when I heard all this noise coming from a deep voice out of the den. I remember asking myself, "Who is that out there barking all that noise?" I decided to get up since my kids were out there and go see. It was one of my sister-in-law's friends, so I just went into the den and sat down. I discovered an interesting phenomenon, all the loud barking from the man with the deep voice stopped. What the young man needed to recognize was that there was another man in the house who appeared to have more authority than he did. Dads, this is why we have to be there.

Attending formal events with my children was also unfamiliar territory. My dad and I would go see boxing matches back in the '70s when Muhammad Ali was fighting Joe Frazier, but we never went to formal affairs together. As the community affairs manager for my company's western region, I go to all kinds of events whether they are formal dinners, star-studded Hollywood productions, award galas or volunteer activities. I often take one of my children as my date. I realized I could not have my wife accompany me to all of these events for a couple of reasons. First, I was working and could not always provide her the attention she deserved and secondly, if she went to all the events that I go to my job would become her job as well. Another thing I realized was that I did not want to be out at events, especially in Los Angeles, being a married man, but appearing to be single. Therefore, I would rotate taking one of the kids as my date and my wife would only attend select events. Now, while this addressed my personal concerns, it also provided my children with opportunities and a breadth of perspective they would not have otherwise experienced and it let them see for themselves what their dad does when I would say I'm going to this or that event. It also answered their questions before they asked them. Little did I know that during this time my children would have the opportunity to meet some of corporate America's brightest leaders and some of Hollywood's brightest stars. Nor did I ever imagine that one of my children would get to meet and work with some of America's great servant leaders, including President Barack Obama.

Not having my dad as a role model, I discovered I had to map out my own plan for handling the years beyond high school and college. I knew that supporting my children's dreams and goals was the right course of action, but I had so many questions. How do you support their undergraduate and postgraduate studies? How do you ensure that their post college dreams are really theirs and not your dreams for them? I am still navigating these uncharted waters as I write this book. Realizing we would have two, possibly three, kids in college at the same time, my wife and I determined long ago that at least 12 years would be lean years for us and we'd have to tighten our belt. Although these have been difficult waters to navigate, as dad, I determined that was the best course of action to take.

Dads often find dealing with young adult children the most troubling stage of parenting. Many dads have a tendency to respond to their young adult children by reacting to the things they do instead of being proactive and setting a course of action for them to follow. When dads react to their kids, particularly their sons, more often than not it's a reaction born out of frustration and/or anger, which often leads them to make decisions that are not always the best. Now, don't think that girls don't do things that make dads react in ways that are not always the best either because they do. It's like the morning I woke up and went out into my garage only to discover that my daughter was in a car accident the night before and totaled the car that I had bought her for college, and, by the way, I never got a phone call. This was the car that I was still paying for so she could attend the college that I was also paying for her to attend. When our children do things like this many dads react in the heat of the moment and make decisions that are often the worse ones we can make. Dads, it is in these moments that you and I have to take a step back and ask, "What is the best decision for the long term regardless of how we feel in the moment?"

My youngest daughter was home for the summer after her first semester of college where she had all the liberty that college students enjoy, however, once home, the lines of liberty shifted. One evening she had gone out to be with some friends and it was getting late so I asked where she was and I was told she went out. Because it was late, I called her to see where she was and she said she was on her way. However, for her, on my way means after a couple of stops and detours. When she arrived home it was well after the hour that I thought she needed to be out, particularly since she was driving her mother's car. As dad, I had to draw the line or else she would continue to take advantage of her new found freedom. After waiting up for her, when she came in I told her that would be the last night I would wait up for her to come home that summer. I don't know how my dad would have handled it, but that's how I did it. She understood the boundaries and we did not have any more problems that summer with her getting home late.

Dads, as you enter those uncharted waters, which are often the most difficult to navigate and for which you don't have a model to emulate, let the biblical model be your compass. General Colin Powell has a book out that is titled "It Worked for Me." Well, dads, the biblical model worked for me to fill those gaps that were left by my dad not being there. Don't let the absence of your dad be an excuse for you not doing it the right way. There are other models that you can learn from:

- The biblical model
- Dads in Scripture
- Faithful men of God
- Other dads with experience
- Read books like this one and others from dads with experience
- Attend workshops and seminars on fatherhood and parenting

Navigating uncharted waters is like white water rafting. Sometimes the waters are smooth and calm, but most of the time, without a professional navigator, they are extremely dangerous. The Bible is clear when it comes to seeking directions and the Scripture says, "Trust in the Lord with all your heart and lean not unto your own understanding, in all your ways acknowledge him, and he will make your paths straight." NIV (Proverbs 3:5-6)

Lessons Learned from Uncharted Waters:

1. Discover a model and chart your course after that model.
2. Chart a course based on love above all things.
3. Models that produce failures teach us what not to do.
4. Successful navigation of uncharted waters can lead to tremendous opportunities and provide a breadth of perspective
5. As with white water rafting, uncharted waters require skillful navigation.
6. Never stop steering the boat, as it were, while trying to navigate uncharted waters.

CHAPTER V

The Danger Zone

The "Danger Zone" represents a time period in a young man or young woman's life when they face a myriad of different and specific dangers. In the United States, I believe the Danger Zone begins in the minority community somewhere around the age of 14 and lasts until about 29 years old. Some of the dangers our young people face in today's society includes, but are not limited to: incarceration, drug use and addiction, unplanned pregnancy, unprepared motherhood and fatherhood, joblessness, hopelessness, gang affiliation, bullying, predators and predatory behaviors, and even death. We live in a country where young boys in the inner cities face the danger of not making it out of those environments. Young men and women face all of these dangers every day of their lives. Growing up in the inner cities of Philadelphia and Columbus, Ohio, our goal was to get out of those environments and have something better. Unfortunately, in our inner cities, there are many young men and women who have never seen their fathers get up and go to work, for whatever reason. Their dad may not live with them or he may be incarcerated or even deceased, so they don't know how that looks. For some of these young men and women, getting up and going to school every day does not seem to be the viable option for gaining success. The fact is, in many cases, gangs and gang activities present what appears to be a more viable option for success, though short-lived at best. Gangs present an acceptable alternative to many of our kids today, both in the inner cities and in the suburbs. They present our kids with a pseudo form of love and acceptance and a place to belong.

Don't think for a minute that because you moved up and out to the suburbs that your kids are safe from these dangers. Since the day our first daughter was born, we have lived in what are called suburban neighborhoods and our kids have faced and still face these dangers on a daily basis. Let me make this as clear as I possibly can – suburban kids face some of the same dangers as inner city kids do every day.

As parents, my wife and I entered the Danger Zone with our children, particularly with our son, as we tried to ensure that we always lived in multicultural communities. The church we attended for most of our kids' lives was located in the heart of the most dangerous zip code in the city of Dallas. As African Americans growing up in the United States, I always wanted them to be well aware of who they were, but I also wanted to balance that with providing them with as safe of an environment as I possibly could. We made sure that we kept our kids connected to communities and schools in which people looked like them, talked like them and acted like them, and, as a result, my son and daughters were faced with the lure of the culture. My son would often come home and say, "Dad, you are not going to believe what just happened." When I asked what, he'd say something like, "I just got stopped by the police!" One time in particular I asked him why did they stop him. He said the officer said the light above the rear tag was out, but when the officer first saw him they were facing one another at the intersection. Every time my son would leave the house, I would wonder: "Is he going to make it back tonight, is this the night that he comes home beaten and battered, is this the night that I get that knock on the door or is this the night or day that I get that phone call that no parent ever wants to receive?" As dads, we have to be there to let our children know that they are accountable. They have to know that they are in the Danger Zone. Recently, I was having lunch with some gentlemen in the community and we were discussing the challenges that many in our community face on a daily basis. I told them that where I live, which is not considered a minority community, my son gets stopped all the time just because he is in the area. I told them that we have had to teach our son how to handle himself in this community when and if he gets stopped. There are house rules in regards to coming and going and all that, and then there are rules about how you conduct yourself when and if you find yourself in one of those "Danger Zone" moments, like a supposedly routine traffic stop. We tell our son to be respectful, keep his hands where they are visible, don't make any sudden moves and say very little. The last thing I want is to see my son or your son on the evening news as the latest statistic.

We often have to have conversations with our kids about the rules pertaining to life outside the house. We want to know specifically when and where they are going. I warn them that house parties today are a bad deal and clubbing can be dangerous. I tell them: "Just because you reach the age of twenty-one doesn't mean that you go bebopping into somebody's club and think that everyone in there is on your side and has your best interest in mind." In today's youth culture there is a need to be connected and socialization has taken on this idea of being "down with your boys"; that is to say having one another's back. This pressure alone is enough to put your children in the Danger Zone. Being "down" with your boys and your boys' boys means when they are in trouble your kid is in trouble, when they are in danger your kid is in danger. Recently, there was a professional athlete who found himself in trouble with the law, as many of them do, and his representative cautioned him about the people who were hanging with him. His representative told him that they didn't have jobs to lose; their job was to keep getting money from him. That's what happens when your kid is "down" with his boys. I vividly recall a time in my own youth when a friend and I had gone to a house party on the other side of town. When we got there I soon realized that the party was in my friend's old neighborhood in which he had grown up. Apparently, while growing up, my friend had been somewhat of a bully to this one particular guy who happened to be the brother of the girl having the party. Well, her brother and his friends had grown into some very big and forceful young men, and I quickly realized that we were most likely going to have to fight our way back to the other side of town. I was in a Danger Zone moment. Fortunately, we got out of that situation with just a lot of talk and threats, largely due to parental intervention. The young man's parents stepped in and would not allow their son and his friends to ruin their daughter's party by giving my friend and I a beat down, which was certain to happen because we were outnumbered, outsized and out of our area of familiarity.

Let me talk about the Danger Zone of drug use and addiction. Today's young people are faced with the lure of the drug culture because drugs have become more plentiful and more available than ever. I spent the first five years of the '80s in college and during this time the United States was reeling from the introduction of crack cocaine. I almost hated to call back home and speak with my brother or sisters because every time I called it seemed like they were telling me horror stories about people with whom I grew up. Stories of guys being set on fire because they owed drug debts; guys I went to school with being gunned down over drug deals, girls being strung out on crack and doing anything to get it. I received a call one evening from a guy I didn't know, but he knew one of my friends who I grew up with and he informed me that she had become what he referred to as a "dollar girl." He told me dollar girls would do anything for one dollar to score drugs. The few times that I would go back to Columbus to visit my family inevitably I would see guys I knew walking the streets and I could hardly recognize them, and some of them were just a few years out of high school; drug use had destroyed them. I used to say they looked like the walking dead. Today's young people are now faced with new drugs, more subtle drugs, but just as dangerous as anything we have ever seen before. Dads, if you are not talking to your sons and daughters about the dangers of drug use you are missing the boat and your kids will pay for your failure to uphold your responsibility in this area.

So, dads, if we know our children are going to go through this period I call the Danger Zone for about 15 years, through adolescence and into young adulthood, how do you and I help them survive the dangers they'll face every day? If we fail to be smart and not provide our children with guidance during this period, some of the decisions they will make will impact them for the rest of their lives. So what are some steps you can take to help them?

Steps to Navigate through the "Danger Zone:"

1. Dads, you have to be there! Dads, you must be a part of your children's lives; there is no substitute for you being there. Let's say that it is physically impossible for you to be there because of decisions you have made or life got in the way, then moms have to find trusted mentors who can be there to help your kids through this period.

2. Secondly, your kids need you in their lives if for no other reason than to have someone who will listen to their ideas and thoughts; even when those ideas or thoughts are not good, especially when the ideas are bad ones and their thoughts are misguided. Dads, we need to become listeners. The problem with adults is that we know so much that we want to keep talking when maybe we should be quiet. The Scripture says in James 1:19-20, "My dear brothers, take note of this: Everyone should be quick to listen, slow to speak and slow to become angry, for man's anger does not bring about the righteous life that God desires." NIV Dads, we need to listen to what our children are saying and what they are not saying so that we know what is going on in their lives.

3. Third, dads, we need to hold our children accountable. Dad, you don't have to be your children's buddy and you don't have to be their pal – you have to be their dad. What does accountability mean? Accountability means that I am going

to hold you to doing what you say you are going to do. In our kids' lives there has to be no way around doing what they say they are going to do. Dads, the reciprocal applies – we have to do what we say we are going to do. There cannot be a double standard; it can't be do as I say not as I do. It amazes me how many parents use drugs, drink alcohol and smoke cigarettes and then act surprised when their kids take up the same habits.

4. Fourth, get a commitment from your children. I know there are pledges that parents sign and have their children sign, agreeing to certain things they will and will not do. While I don't have a problem with that approach if it works for you, my experience has been that in the African American community that approach does not necessarily work. But, dads, we have to get commitments from our children. Our sons and daughters have to know that they will be respectful, starting with respecting themselves and then respecting others. Fathers who have sons, you have to get a commitment from your sons that they will respect women, and that starts at home with them respecting their mother and their sisters. In our house you didn't get to disrespect one another without consequences. Respect was and is an expectation.

5. Fifth, dads, you have to follow up. You must follow up often to make sure your kids did what they said they were going to do. One of the greatest blessings that my wife and I receive from time to time is when someone tells us they saw one of our kids in public and he or she was so respectful. People have told us they saw our son holding the door for a senior citizen or helping someone in need. Others have told us they observed our daughters speaking publicly or doing something in public that reflected well on their mother's home training.

6. Build in expectations! Our kids know beyond a shadow of any doubt that there are built in expectations for them. They

know that they represent my wife and I and they represent the Gibbs name. Sometimes I think my kids view me as the most successful person they know. Sure, they know people who have much more money than we do and they certainly know people who have achieved more than we have, but still they think that we have had a successful life. So there is an expectation that they, too, will be successful. I believe we have to build in those expectations. If we don't expect anything of them, why would they do anything? One of the saddest things you will ever see is a child without any expectations. Dads, you have to build in expectations that your kids will get an education, you have to build in expectations about who they will date, and you have to build expectations that they will choose their friends and associates wisely. For example, my daughters know that coming home dragging a "roughneck" behind them is not acceptable. Dads, our children have to know that their choices affect more than just themselves. That's why a roughneck is not part of our expectation equation, because he or she becomes a problem for our child and the entire family. Dads, if you don't have high expectations for your children you are cheating them out of your wisdom and experience. We expect our kids to make sound decisions based on the best judgment and wisdom they have learned from us and other wise people in their lives.

7. Give them an alternative not an ultimatum. One of the realities that I face having a bi-vocational career of manager and minister is the fact that my kids are preacher's kids aka "PK's." As such, there are some things that I don't agree with and don't believe in that society says are OK to do. Consequently, when our kids were growing up they wanted and needed alternatives. For example, if we didn't believe in celebrating a particular holiday we would plan another activity. When I told my kids that they couldn't do this or

that, I needed to offer them other options. We decided to focus on cultural enrichment. That is one of the reasons we began taking vacations. On the way to Disney World they saw for the first time orange groves along the highways of Florida; they saw the majestic Sedona National Park, often called "Red Rock Country"; they saw the beauty of the Grand Canyon and the rushing mighty Colorado River; they saw the Hoover Dam and learned how it was built; on the way to St. Louis Missouri they ate at the world's largest McDonalds; while in Washington, DC they saw the great monuments and historical treasures of this great nation, while in New York City they stood in Time Square and visited some of the world's most famous named stores and brands; and in Atlanta, the mecca of the South, they saw the Coca Cola Building and CNN.

Did providing them with alternatives cost me? Absolutely, it cost me a lot, but it was worth every penny. Dads, providing our kids with alternatives meant someone had to sacrifice something and more often than not that someone was dad. Maybe I couldn't buy that new suit or new pair of shoes or maybe I didn't get that luxury car. The truth be told, early on, I shopped at resale stores for some of my suits and I normally had my shoes resoled a couple times before buying new ones. These were just a few of the sacrifices that I made so my kids would have positive alternatives. Dads, if you want to help your kids get through the Danger Zone you have to make it so that they want to be around you, you have to make it so that they believe being around dad is not that bad, but, in fact, it pays dividends hanging out with dad. I am reminded of the biblical character Job who said the one thing he missed out of all that he had was not having his children around him. (Job 29:5) Job lost everything, but his greatest loss was the closeness that he shared with his children. In all that I have said, the most important thing is that you have to be there; your presence in your kids' lives is and will continue to be the difference maker throughout the Danger Zone. Dads, the Scripture is clear on this point. It says we are to train up children in the way they should go and although they may stray when they get older they will not depart from what we taught them. Our kids are going to make some wrong, and even bad, decisions along the way, but our training and influence will make a difference, provided we don't relinquish our responsibilities to today's culture or to someone else.

8. Know what your kids are doing. This means that as dads you have to go look. Dad, go look! What does that mean? In our house I pay the mortgage every month, which gives me the right and access to every room, every closet, every cabinet and every drawer. There are times when I use my access key liberally, but there should come a time when you no longer have to use your access key at all because not only is the trust built up but the respect for the home is also established. We had a rule in our house that nothing was brought into our home for which there was not a receipt. We didn't buy things from places or people who couldn't provide us with a sales receipt. You couldn't buy things with the "hook up" because I wanted to know where things came from and were they purchased legitimately and from a legitimate establishment. I wanted to avoid the danger of someone coming and knocking on my door asking about something in my house. I told my son a long time ago that I would not be an Eli, meaning I would not stand by and let him destroy himself and let him destroy what God has given us and not say something and do something about it.

Dads, you can get your children through the Danger Zone, but you have to take some decisive steps to ensure that they don't become ensnared during this difficult and tumultuous period. This period is not a one summer ordeal or a one semester crisis; it's a 10-year deal at best. As a father of three I am still going through the Danger Zone with our two youngest children. Although they are young adults, they are not completely through this period so my wife and I have to stay vigilant to maintain our responsibilities as it pertains to them.

According to the U.S. Department of Justice there are more than seven million people who are under supervision of the adult correctional system.[5] Between probation, parole, jail, and state and federal prison, more than seven million people in the United States alone got snared by something in the Danger Zone. According to the Justice Department report, minorities, Blacks and Hispanic/Latinos make up a disproportionate number of those who have landed in the adult correctional system. Dads, if we relinquish our responsibility, what's going to keep our kids from adding to these statistics? Make the sacrifice, give your kids an alternative verses an ultimatum. You can make it through the Danger Zone, but it takes hard work and commitment to being there in your children's lives. The Danger Zone is something I think about every day of my life, every time my son leaves the house, when we send our daughter back to college for another semester, and when we launched our oldest daughter to start her career. As a dad, my spiritual antenna is always on alert for the dangers that threaten their lives. Now, so you don't think I am paranoid, let me say that my life's Scripture verses for the last 40 years have been Psalm 37:3-4, which says, "Trust in the Lord and do good; dwell in the land and enjoy **safe** pasture. Delight yourself in the Lord and he will give you the desires of your heart." NIV This is not to say that something can't happen, but I am trusting God that it will not happen. When I do my part of what these verses say, God is obligated to do his part of what his word says. Dads, we ought to pray a prayer of protection for our children every day. Jesus said to his disciples when he was in the Garden of Gethsemane, "Watch and pray so that you will not fall into temptation. The spirit is willing, but the body is weak." NIV (Matthew 26:41; Mark 14:38; Luke 22:46)

Lessons Learned from the Danger Zone:

1. Dads must recognize precisely when their children enter the Danger Zone.
2. Dads must prepare their children for life in the Danger Zone.
3. Don't be afraid to share your own Danger Zone experiences with your children when applicable.
4. Be real with your children as it pertains to the potential dangers they may face.
5. Remember to always apply the eight steps of navigating the Danger Zone:
    a. Be there!
    b. Listen
    c. Accountability
    d. Commitment
    e. Follow up!
    f. Expectations
    g. Alternatives
    h. Awareness
9. Lastly, dads, never relinquish your responsibility to help them navigate the Danger Zone.

CHAPTER VI

Career Advancement — The House of Cards

Many years ago, my pastor and mentor Dr. Lane and I were having one of many conversations that we had about careers and how to navigate through a bi-vocational career. It was a very normal conversation that we would have from time to time because we were both bi-vocational. He was the senior pastor of our church and he was a professor at Dallas Theological Seminary. Although he working for the seminary was nothing like me working for UPS, they presented similar challenges to family life and raising children. When you are a well sought after pastor and seminary professor you are presented with opportunities to go different places, be involved in different ministry opportunities and be a servant of God all over the world. You have to decide which opportunities are good opportunities and which ones you cannot afford to accept. My pastor once compared it to a house of cards. As you build a house of cards it is imperative that each card is positioned just right so that it can hold the weight of the next card that you will place on top of it. Not only does each card require exact placement, but when you pull a card out of the house you have to ensure that it's not a card that will cause the whole house to collapse. For example, when you are making career decisions you have to make sure that you don't make a decision that is money driven without considering the cost of that decision. Not everything that is good is good for you! Therein lies the need for the wisdom of God to teach us how and to lead us through the process of building our proverbial house of cards. If you recall, I told you earlier that one of the pieces of advice my dad gave me was to consider the end of a thing before I started it, well that advice applied to my house of cards as I built my career. The gospel writer of the book of Luke in 14:28 says, "Suppose one of you wants to build a tower. Will he not first sit down and estimate the cost to see if he has enough money to complete it?" NIV

Building a career that spans more than three decades with one company in most cases is a thing of the past. UPS is one of the few companies where that is still possible. Although we cannot predict what will happen in the future as we continue to build this house made of cards. Dads, as you and I build our careers we have to always be mindful that we are building, as it were, a house of cards. What is the card that you can least afford to pull out and your house remains strong? As in the building of a house to live in, what wall is a load-bearing wall that is holding up the structure of the house? Oftentimes, we make career decisions or allow someone else to make career decisions for us without counting the cost as the writer of Luke suggested that good builders do. Many companies have different career development processes that they use to provide advancement opportunities to their employees; we only hope that they spend time evaluating the cost to families. For years at our company people usually said yes to whatever assignment they were asked to take. It was a culture in which people just didn't say no when asked to take on a new or different responsibility. That was the company I grew up in, but somewhere along the way things began to shift and people began to say: not at this time, it's not right for me and my family, we have relocation restrictions, that's not the direction in which I am looking for my career to go, what will that assignment do for me and my career, and that's simply not something I want to do. However, this new way of responding was not the culture that was engrained in me over three decades.

In August of 2007 when I received that call from my manager and was informed that there may be an opportunity for me in the Pacific Region I said, "I'll go." The following Wednesday morning I was on the first flight from Dallas to Orange County, California.

Did I take time to count the cost, absolutely! However, the cost that I focused on was not the cost of relocating so much as I counted the cost of staying in Dallas. Saying no in my mind meant a few sure things: it would close the door for future career opportunities; secondly, it would no doubt have led to a reclassification at some point; and third, it would mean that our family would be deprived the growth opportunities associated with relocations. Over the years people had told me that when they relocated their family for their careers oftentimes their families drew closer together because they had to depend upon one another. There were also relocation horror stories where it didn't work out so well, kids didn't adjust, spouses couldn't adjust and on rare occasions the employee did not adjust. But for me no was not an option, I had to move forward if I wanted to finish the last third of my career with dignity and respect.

Dads, when you make the decision to relocate your family do more than count the cost of selling a home and purchasing a new home, count the cost to your family. For me the costs of both were extremely high. Let me explain, when that call came from my manager, school for the kids had already started. Our youngest was beginning the ninth grade, the first official year of high school, but our son was starting his senior year in high school, and I still said yes. How does a father decide to relocate his family in one of his children's most important years of school? He does it by counting up the cost. By the way, the oldest child was starting her junior year in college. And, coincidentally, the country was headed for one of the worse recessions since the Great Depression of 1929. The first thing I decided to do was to exhibit a confident, determined, unshakeable faith in the power of God to do everything that His word says that He can and will do. In spite of how I got to the point of relocation, that's where we were and I was trusting that God would not begin failing me at this most critical time in our lives.

I immediately went into a period of sober thinking with much prayer, fasting and seeking God's direction. My dilemma was I needed to sell a house in order to buy a house during a recession. The housing market was declining faster than most people realized. Our beautiful five bedroom custom home should have sold in no time for a fair market value, but no one was buying. Realtors were low-balling their prices. They valued our home nearly $100,000 under our original asking price. Housing costs in California were in the high six figures; sellers were trying to hold their property values as high as possible although the market was dragging them down. My relocation clock was ticking. My house wasn't selling, buying was looking grim, and my son was well into his senior year. There came a critical point in which I had to decide what price I was willing to pay to continue advancing my career. The decision was made, we would buy in California and the family would stay in Dallas until our son graduated from high school. That meant carrying two mortgages, one for the Dallas home where the family lived while he finished school and the California home where we would all live once he graduated. On the surface the price was that of two sizable mortgages, which was bearable for a short period of time, but the real cost was being away from my family for nine months. Dads, if you think for one minute that your presence in the home does not matter, let me say that you are woefully mistaken, your presence matters. During that nine month period a lot of things began to go terribly wrong. On one occasion the two kids who were at home in Dallas were not acting right and things seemed to be spiraling out of control and all I wanted to do was to be there and put things back in order, but I couldn't without incurring some type of backlash and career consequences. On this particular morning I had gotten up to call the kids to make sure they were up for school and things were just not good at all; they were not acting like the kids that we raised. As I prayed that morning, I told the Lord that I was ready to give up a 28-year career and go home and fix my family. As I sat there on the edge of the hotel bed praying, I was interrupted by a text message from one of the church ministers, Reverend Emanuel Holloman, encouraging me to remain strong in faith. Little did he know, but it was at that moment that my faith was being challenged like never before. I replied to him and told him that I was ready to give up and quit. He didn't wait, he didn't send me another text message, he picked up the phone and called me. That call saved my career because I was about to call my boss and tell her I was going back to Dallas because this was not working out.

Not long after that critical turning point things began to fall into place until it was time for the family to move. I went home that June to be a part of our son's graduation ceremonies and to prepare the family for the move to California. I had already brought one car to California and so it was a matter of getting the other two cars moved and getting the family on a plane. Oh, that it was so easy! A week before the scheduled move, the transmission in my son's car died and had to be rebuilt. If you remember when we were discussing uncharted waters I told you about the time I went into the garage to discover a totaled automobile, well that was the week we were scheduled to move. So in the scope of two weeks we went from having enough transportation for everyone who was driving at the time to being severally transportation challenged. We let our daughter take her mother's car back to Atlanta to finish college, we got our son's transmission rebuilt and just days after his graduation ceremonies we moved. My wife and daughter flew out to California and my son and I drove his car 1,500 miles from Dallas to Orange County, California. For 700 miles he did not say a word, which was a heavy price to pay.

If the story ended here, you might say what a miserable experience, but it doesn't. Within two weeks of being in California my son came to me and said, "You know, dad, California isn't that bad." I think all it took was a couple trips to the beach. However, from my vantage point, life was not about the California beaches, ocean and mountains all around you. For me, it was about how do you make this work for your good. Our daughter began playing high school volleyball, and at the first awards banquet, school administrators announced the seniors, their grade point averages and where they planned to attend college. To my surprise and I believe our daughter's surprise, her teammates were graduating with grade point averages in the high threes and mid fours. I think that experience really ignited a spark in our daughter and she realized that while she was in Dallas she was an honor student performing at an average level. Within a few months, the fire was burning within her and she started to perform at the level that we both knew she was capable. She went on the graduate with honors and has continued to maintain a high grade point average into her third year of college; even to the point of earning academic scholarship rewards. Our daughter went to school out of state, but because of her academic performance we paid in-state tuition. She also received additional scholarships and rewards. I have to share this one quick story about one of her scholarships. Our daughter was awarded a particular scholarship and the finance office did not have record of the award ever arriving at the school. I called the organization that provided the award to let them know that it had not arrived and they informed me that the school was mistaken and the award was in fact there at the school. So, I told the gentlemen there was one thing he could be assured of and that was that Tracey would not disappoint them. His reply was one of those proud dad moments. He said, "Mr. Gibbs, I have spoken with Tracey a number of times and from the first time I spoke with her over the phone I could tell that she would not disappoint us, and we are so proud to be able to award her this scholarship."

When we first relocated to California, I wanted to make sure that we were able to provide a trainer for our son so that he could continue to develop his skills as a basketball player. However, I knew with all the additional mortgage and transportation expenses a trainer was a luxury I just couldn't afford. I was talking with one of the guys at church one day and he told me he trained kids every day in speed and conditioning and that he would love to work with my son. Sam Reed began training Nathan every day and never once charged me a penny. On another occasion a coach was in the gym conducting practice with the women's basketball team and there were some guys from the men's team being disrespectful, and Nathan called them out for disrespecting the game and the coach. When the coach saw him exhibiting that type of leadership, he told him that he liked that and he wanted to work with him and provide him with skills training. For months, he, too, gave Nathan one-on-one skills training and never asked for a penny. By the way, God didn't just provide Nathan with people who believed in him and were willing to help him, but God rewarded him by allowing his team to win a California State Basketball Title in the 2010/2011 season. Not only did he win the title but he received a Division 1 scholarship and later a full scholarship to play at Westmont College in Santa Barbara, California. Also, he went to Manila in the Philippines to work on a short-term mission with Kids International Ministries and has since had the opportunity to play professional in Germany and Denmark.

Our oldest daughter Courtney graduated from Clark Atlanta University in 2009 in the middle of this country's Great Recession and, like so many others, could not find employment. I could no longer afford to keep her in an apartment because we already had two mortgages. My advice to her was to come to California and re-launch after the recession, but for the time being we would keep all the money in one household. She took my advice and moved to California and immediately found a job. Although she found a job, it was not in her field of study and she was not happy. Once again, I knew I had to make my recommendations carefully less she reject them and decide to do her own thing. So I recommended that she do what I saw many others doing; take advantage of this time in a down economy and go back to school and obtain her postgraduate degree. She took my advice and earned a master's degree at Cal State University, Long Beach. As she was near completion of her master's degree, she had an opportunity to work on the 2012 Presidential Reelection Campaign of President Barack Obama. For me, it was a no-brainer. The next chapter will cover the reelection campaign in detail, but for now let me just say that the story – and opportunities – could have ended long ago had I just said no to relocating.

There are times when people present you with opportunities, but they don't necessarily have your best interest at heart. Like in the case of the Jewish patriarch Jacob's son, Joseph; his brothers had one intention when they sold him into slavery, but God had a completely different plan.

Dads, when I counted up the cost, although I could have never predicted what would happen, but based on historical and empirical data I could predict what would have happened had we stayed in Dallas. What we have experienced since relocating to California, for all intense and purposes, was supposed to crush us, but it did not. In 2011/2012 we had all three kids in college, that was supposed to destroy us financially, but it did not; in 2010 my job was reclassified and that was supposed to annihilate us, but it did not; my income remained stagnate from 2008 through 2013 which should have broken my proverbial financial back, but it did not. I'm not telling you these very personal details to boast about how spiritual I am, but I share these things for one reason and one reason only and that is to let some dad know that with God all things are possible and you can trust Him to do exactly what His word says He will do. Regardless of how dismal things may appear, when you place your faith in Jesus Christ, who is the author and finisher of our faith, you cannot lose. It's obvious that I don't know details about the readers of this book, but I know a little about what God has said and I know that there is no situation and there are no circumstances in which God cannot make a difference. Your career decisions should not be left out of his hands. Just as God wants to have a personal relationship with you in every other area of your life, he is very interested in what you do with one of the largest segments of your life which is your work and your career.

Lessons Learned from Career Advancement:

1. Dads, "Count the cost!"
2. Understand your company's culture as it pertains to career development.

3. Godly careers are built on confident, determined, unshakeable faith in the power of God.
4. Career decisions impact the family as much if not more than they do the employee.
5. Career decisions that remove the father's presence from the home, while they may appear to benefit an organization, they can destroy a family.
6. Dads, how you get somewhere is one thing, what God does with you in the process is a totally different story.
7. The Lord knows the plans he has for you and your career decisions should not be left out of his hands.

CHAPTER VII

The Presidential Reelection Campaign

So what does the presidential reelection campaign have to do with the heart of a dad? As preachers often say in their homilies to such rhetorical questions "I'm glad you asked." In April of 2012 I was hosting a number of dinner guests at one of the many community events that I attend in connection with the work that I do and one of my dinner guests, a woman named Mrs. Lena Kennedy, asked me about my kids and what they would be doing for the summer. Now, if you want to have a conversation with me, ask me about my kids; at some point you may have to say OK, George, that's enough. Mrs. Kennedy, who worked on President Obama's Finance Committee for his reelection campaign, asked if I thought any of my kids would be interested in working on the campaign. My first thought was who are we that one of our children might have the opportunity to be engaged in the political process in such a capacity? Although we have followed politics throughout many elections, we had never been what you would call closely engaged in any particular political campaign. However, I thought about our oldest daughter and the fact that she has a heart for the community and helping organizations, so I suggested that she might be interested, but said I would need to ask her. I was not at all surprised when my daughter said she was interested in finding out what the work would entail.

Finding out what the work would entail was the start of a new journey not only for Courtney but the entire family, extended family included. The journey began with her having to complete a training class to be considered as an applicant. The two-week training period overlapped with the last two weeks of her completing her master's program. During this two-week period in May 2012 Courtney had a number of assignments to complete for both her degree and the campaign applicant training. She also received an invitation to attend The Women for Obama Conference, which was held in Washington, D.C. On top of all this, she still maintained her full-time job because there was no guarantee that she would get the job on the campaign team. In short, she finished the campaign training assignments, her master's degree program and she attended the conference.

It was during this extremely challenging time in Courtney's life that my support as dad became very critical. We had conversations at every step in the process. We talked about what it would mean when it became time for her to give up her job that she had held since moving to California and taking on a job that we knew would last only four to six months, but may give her the experience of a lifetime and may be the launch pad for the start of her career. We talked about the wisdom of attending the conference in the middle of completing the campaign training and finishing up the work for her master's degree. Once the opportunity was presented, I suggested she attend the conference; I felt it would benefit her more than it would hinder her. She took my advice and went to the conference. Little did she know that the president would make a guest appearance and not only would she get to see and hear him, but she would be one of the people on the front line who would get the opportunity to shake hands with him. While at the conference, Courtney met a group of women who asked her to take pictures of President Obama, which led to her being at the front of the room and gave her the opportunity to take photos of the president shaking hands with a little girl, and it was at that point that the president also shook her hand. My daughter being in close proximity to the president of the United States and having the opportunity that was presented to her was more than we could have ever imagined.

Courtney returned from the conference with a renewed sense of excitement and enthusiasm, and once the campaign applicant training was finished, the phone started ringing. (By the way, attending the conference actually enabled her to complete a number of assignments.) While the economy was still sluggish and companies were restructuring, right-sizing, transforming or whatever title they wanted to put on it, the Presidential Reelection Campaign was hiring. Several battleground state campaign offices called to ask Courtney to come work on the campaign. The Colorado office called and the Nevada office called, but the Ohio campaign office was very persistent. For me, Ohio was a no-brainer: my family lived in Ohio, I grew up in Ohio; Courtney would have a support system in Ohio and it would give her an opportunity to build closer bonds with my side of the family. Because our kids grew up in Texas they did not get to visit their extended family in Ohio as often as we would have liked. The general rule is if you want to stay happily married as long as Teresa and I have been married you go visit your wife's family as often as you can, which means you may visit your side of the family only on occasion. The Ohio campaign office made Courtney an offer she just could not refuse. Not only did they place her within driving distance of the family, but they provided supportive housing for the campaign team. My wife and I are forever grateful to Patricia who opened up her home to Courtney for six months while she worked on the campaign.

The Ohio Connection

As a dad, I had some anxiety about the uncertainty of what she would be doing and there were times when I was actually concerned about her safety as she was out canvassing in the middle of a very contentious political climate and campaign. I knew that much of the "political silliness," as the president liked to call it, was spilling over into the campaigns in the streets. That being said, I was still 100 percent confident that we made the absolute right decision to encourage her to go and be a part of the political process.

Courtney and I talked nearly every day while she was in Dayton, where her campaign team was assigned. One of the first things we learned was that running a political campaign was not an eight-hour workday. Courtney soon discovered that some days the work began early in the morning and did not end until late in the evening. Her typical day was anywhere from 10 to 16 hours, six days a week. In fact, on several occasions while Courtney and her team were out canvassing they were criticized for being "out-of-towners" who were taking jobs from local residents. People wanted to know why the campaign officials brought in "out-of-towners." To help Courtney put things into perspective, I asked her were the people who needed jobs willing to do the job she was doing. Were they willing to build volunteer campaign teams to canvas the streets of Dayton every day come rain or shine? Were they willing to work all day and then half the night to finish an assignment? Were they willing to work six to seven days a week for no extra pay? Were they willing to meet the goals that she was tasked with weekly? Would those people who needed jobs be willing to work the month of October leading up to the election with only one day off and that day was filled with meetings? Once she had a clearer perspective, Courtney no longer let the noise about being an "out-of-towner" trouble her.

Working on the Presidential Reelection Campaign Team was certainly an area of uncharted waters, not only for Courtney but for the rest of us as well. However, I could not have been more proud of our daughter during that six-month period. When Courtney moved to Ohio, she had to basically start from scratch. While the campaign infrastructure was in place and the process was in place to bring about a successful campaign, the work of canvassing neighborhoods still had to be done. Courtney had to build her own campaign teams within the overall state campaign team. I told you earlier that we always lived in areas that were culturally diverse, but we had social and religious involvement in what would be considered urban neighborhoods, so when it became time for Courtney to canvas some of the most challenging areas of the city she was not afraid to engage people. In the African American community there are three institutions that are of primary importance: Historically Black

Colleges and Universities, black churches and hair establishments. Dayton does not have a HBCU, so Courtney built her strategy around black churches, hair salons, barbershops and other civic organizations. Although these groups were all important to the campaign, they each posed a different set of challenges for her to gain their cooperation. However, every day she would tell me about the challenges and we would talk about how to overcome them or how she had already overcome the challenge.

One of the constant challenges she faced during the campaign was getting people to believe that their voice mattered and that their vote was important. Montgomery County is a rather small county of about 500,000 people and Dayton is not the main attraction of Ohio. Although my dad often took my brother and I to Dayton to watch boxing matches on the big screen in the arena, in the general landscape of Ohio politics, Dayton while important is not Columbus where the state capital is, or Cleveland or Cincinnati. When you think of Ohio you think of the three C's – Columbus, Cleveland and Cincinnati. So the challenge was how to get Dayton and Montgomery County residents enthused about the political process and the campaign. It was determined that they needed a surrogate to come to Dayton and help rally the city. The team was given just a few days' notice that First Lady Michelle Obama would be coming to Dayton for a campaign rally. Courtney's office had primary responsibilities for getting the word out and getting people there. This presented many opportunities for her to activate her team members, demonstrate her leadership skills and show her appreciation to those who had been helping her during the campaign. I always wondered how you get to be one of those people down front at one of these events and now I know; you have to be involved and have a vested interest in the event.

For Courtney, the First Lady's visit to Dayton was bittersweet. Her boss thought so much of her leadership skills that he asked her to be

> *Another*
> *Proud*
> *Moment*

a part of the setup team at the site of the rally, so she went to the site along with her team of volunteers and helped to set up. While she was at the rally site, the First Lady made a surprise visit to their campaign office. Needless to say, Courtney was disappointed that she did not get to meet her. However, she did get to see and hear her at the campaign rally. Not only did Courtney get to see the First Lady, but her grandmother and aunts and supporters were given the opportunity to sit up front. To have my daughter involved at that level created another of those proud moments that being a dad has afforded me.

Opportunity Knocked

Working on the campaign afforded Courtney a number of opportunities to not only meet significant people in the campaign, but it also presented her with opportunities to continually demonstrate her ability to provide leadership. I told you that barbershops and beauty salons are staples in the African American community, so on one occasion Courtney called to tell me that she would be introducing Grammy Award-winning singer-songwriter John Legend in one of the shops that had been supporting her. The next thing I knew my phone is buzzing with pictures of her standing next to Legend, introducing him to the crowd of people who had come out to see him. Legend is a native of Springfield, Ohio, just 25 miles from Dayton. Shop owners soon began to realize that there were fringe benefits to letting this "out-of-towner" take up residence in their shops and register their patrons to vote. This, too, was a proud moment. Later, Courtney had the opportunity to visit with Democratic National Committee Chairperson Rep. Debbie Wasserman Schultz at the campaign office, along with Valerie B. Jarrett, who is a senior advisor to President Obama. Once again, my phone was buzzing with photos.

On another occasion, Courtney called to tell me that they had gotten word that President Obama was coming to Dayton, along with Vice President Biden. She was so excited that the president and vice president were coming to Dayton and she would get to be a part of the event. Vice President Biden had made a prior campaign stop in Dayton, but Courtney and most of the campaign staff was not able to attend his rally because they were out canvassing and strengthening their ground support. To have the president coming was very exciting to say the least. Courtney took the opportunity to splurge and buy a new suit to wear during his visit. Unfortunately, her excitement was tempered when her campaign office manager informed her that she may not get to be a part of the event because he had a special project for her. While disappointed, once again, she was committed to the reelection of the president and that superseded the prospect of not seeing him. Her boss told her he needed her to drive one of the vans that carried staffers. Well, it turned out that the van she was assigned to drive was carrying members of the Presidential Press Core. This meant that where the president went they went. The van was also a part of the presidential motorcade. Once again, several family members, including my mother, her grandmother and aunts, and many of her supporters, including people from the beauty salons, barbershops and churches, were given the opportunity to attend the campaign rally that featured President Obama and Vice President Biden on stage together. Courtney, on the other hand, was driving the van carrying the Presidential Press Core in the motorcade. She was so excited and we were so proud of her.

When the press core arrived at the airport they were given security instructions to stay together; that meant where the president went they went. Courtney and others who would be in the motorcade awaited the president on the tarmac as Air Force One landed. She took photos of Air Force One and photos of her standing next to the presidential limousine. As the motorcade traveled through town on the way to the rally, crowds lined the streets and overpasses cheering on the presidential motorcade, of which Courtney was significant member. When they arrived at the event, although Courtney was not out in the audience, she was behind the scene in a private area with the press core and the president. Courtney said President Obama took time and spoke with each member of the campaign team and thanked them for their service on the campaign, shook their hands, asked them about themselves and then took individual photos with them all. Although Courtney sent a backstage photo of the president shaking hands to my phone, the photo I looked forward to having was the official one of her with the president of the United States. We could not have been happier for our daughter than we were on that day. When she called me she was so excited she could hardly contain herself. I shared the excitement that we both felt with my colleagues in the office; I think I was sharing the pride of being her dad more than anything. Supporters and non-supporters of the president celebrated with me because it really was not about the president, it was about the pride and joy of being her dad.

During the months that Courtney worked on the campaign, Teresa and I talked about how nice it would be for us to be in Ohio with our daughter on election night, but we knew it would be very difficult for us both to make the trip and neither of us wanted to go alone. Teresa was recovering from foot surgery, and we had just paid another semester of college tuition; it just didn't seem like it was going to happen. However, tragedy has a way of changing our perspective on what's important. On October 28, 2012, I received a call from my younger sister telling me that one of my young cousins, who was just 18 years old, had been shot and killed the night before. What was important immediately shifted; I knew it was now important that we go to Ohio to be with the family, and they asked us to come home. My wife and I made arrangements to go to Columbus the weekend leading up to the election because my cousin's funeral service was scheduled for the Monday before Election Day. When my wife and I arrived in Columbus we met with the family to wrap our minds around the events that occurred and figure out the plans for the weekend. We knew we needed to be very supportive of our family and recognize their need for comforting, but we also knew we needed to be there for our daughter. On Saturday night we attended a candlelight vigil that the kids from my cousin's high school had organized. This provided me the opportunity to minister to my cousin's friends; so many of whom were trying to somehow assume a level of responsibility for what happened to her. My heart was bleeding for her mother and father and grandparents who prematurely lost their child. Although it happens every day, no parent should ever have to bury a child; especially as a result of a senseless act of violence.

On Sunday everybody went to church, whichever church they normally attended, and later that afternoon we had a family dinner at a rented space that was large enough to hold the entire family who had come in from all over the country; from California to the Carolinas and from Philadelphia to Texas and everywhere in between. This gave me another opportunity to minister to the entire family and have prayer. After the family dinner, Teresa and I drove up to Dayton to be with Courtney. It was amazing to see her in action; she was in full campaign organizing mode. In fact, she put Teresa and me to work organizing canvassing packets; we must have stayed there until well after midnight. On Monday we spent the day with the family at the funeral service and later that evening we visited with family members we had not seen in some time. On Tuesday, which was Election Day, my sister-in-law joined Teresa and I on our trip back to Dayton to be with our daughter. However, because she was so busy working, we did not see her until after the polls closed that evening. That doesn't mean she didn't put us to work though; she left instructions with her volunteer staff as to what we were supposed to do once we arrived.

That evening after the polls closed, we had our first opportunity to meet the campaign supporter who hosted Courtney for the several months that she worked on the campaign. Later on we all went to the Election Night Watch Party to see and hear the results of the campaign. The Election Night Watch Party was electrifying; it was like nothing that I had ever seen before in my life. Every time a state was called for President Obama the crowd erupted. If you recall, for most of the evening the president was trailing his opponent until the western states began to be called, at which time the president took a commanding lead. When the president took the lead the crowd erupted, but when the news outlets called Hamilton County, where Cincinnati is, the crowd's jubilation was over the top. I was thinking to myself why are these people getting this excited, he still has not won the state. I grew up in Franklin County and I knew Franklin County was much larger than Hamilton County, but what I didn't know was that the data projected that if the president won Hamilton, Franklin and Cuyahoga counties it was a pretty sure bet that he would win the state of Ohio. These three counties comprised the three C's: Columbus, Cleveland and Cincinnati. Not long after the news outlets called Hamilton County, they began calling the state of Ohio for the president, which provided him with the Electoral College votes needed to win reelection. When they called the state of Ohio for the president the joy and elation in that place was unbelievable. When that moment occurred my daughter came to me and hugged me like she has never hugged me before. She cried and I cried and we cried together; not just because the president was winning, but it was an accumulation of moments that we had shared over the several months that she worked on the campaign. Moments that resulted in the successful outcome of the president being reelected. All the hard work, getting up early, staying up late, knocking on doors, being told no, being told what she could not do, and being criticized – all came to a head in that moment. I was so proud of her and so thankful that we had the opportunity to be there and share in this special moment with our daughter.

While I regret the circumstances that led us to be in Ohio during the election, I am so thankful that we were there. Being there with our daughter was about supporting her and the work she had been doing for 10 to 16 hours a day for several months of her life. When people ask me how I do some of the things that I do with and for our kids, I say it's never about how, it's always about why. How is never the question for me; the question for me always starts with why? When I answer why, how is just a matter of logistics. Why is for moments like those I experienced with our daughter the night the president was reelected. As dad, it was important for me to be there, and, as dad, it is important for you to be there in your children's lives. Being there is not cheap or inexpensive, it cost to be there, and, dad, it will cost you to be in your children's lives. For me and my wife to pick up and fly from California to Ohio with a few days' notice cost us tremendously, but it was worth every penny. Dads, no matter the cost, there are times that you and I just have to be there for our children. Our daughter is stronger because she went through this experience, we are stronger for having gone through this experience, and our family is stronger because of it. Courtney, whether she knew it at the time or not, influenced the actions of her siblings and others with whom she grew up. I began to hear comments like: "Courtney is doing her thing, I better get busy doing mine." In fact, she motivated me to get going with this book.

My challenge to dads who are reading this book is to be dad and come through for your children. Yes, it will cost you, but you must be there and come through for your children. They are counting on you. If you want to experience great moments with your children you have to be there supporting them. When our youngest daughter says she just called to tell me about what happened at church or in school today, she needs me to be there to share in her experience. When our son comes to me and says he just wanted me to know that he's still trusting that God is going to see him through and work things out for his good and God's glory, he needs me to be there to share in his experience. Your kids expect you to be there to listen to their hopes, their dreams, their aspirations. Dads, you will never experience these moments if you are not there. It's not enough for you to write a check and think that everything is OK; it's not enough for you to see your kids on weekends or in the summer and around holidays. Now, I realize that for some of you that's all you have and maybe that's all the courts will allow, but I am saying it's not enough.

We can't unscramble the egg and you have what you have, but I am simply saying when you choose not be in your kids' lives, it tends to be a recipe for failure, and by the way, it's your loss. I recently heard it said that if you think the cost of education is expensive, the cost of ignorance is greater. Well, let me put it this way, if you think the cost of being in your children's lives is a high price to pay, the cost of not being in their lives is greater.

Dads, if you do nothing else, you need to find a way to legitimately be a part of your children's lives. And my final thoughts are for those dads who have and are planting seeds all over the place, and you know what I mean. God will hold you responsible for every seed that you deposit and every child that is born as a result of your actions. While I am not casting judgment upon anyone, I am simply saying that God holds each of us accountable for our actions. So the choice really is yours, you can have great moments of joy and pain being in your children's lives or you can have greater moments of pain and unhappiness by not being in your children's lives. The choice is yours!

Lessons Learned from the Presidential Re-election Campaign:

1. Opportunity seized leads to opportunities provided.
2. Dad's support of his children's endeavors is critical to their success.
3. Dad's advice is critical to children's success.
4. Dad's enthusiasm is critical to children's confidence.
5. Dad's support creates family bonding opportunities.
6. Your children are capable of giving you more pride and joy than you could ever imagine was possible.
7. Dads, your children have unborn skills and abilities waiting to be discovered.

8. Our children gain strength through overcoming challenges on their own when they know that we have their back.

9. Dads, when required you have to come through for your children.

10. Don't let the opportunity to become a part of something special in your child's life pass you by.

PART TWO

Parenting Lessons Learned from Biblical Fathers

CHAPTER VIII

Lessons Learned from Adam — The Start of Parenting (Genesis 4)

When I am preparing to deliver a message or make some type of public presentation or I'm just studying for my personal edification and/or enjoyment, I like to go back to the beginning of the subject or the beginning of the chapter so that I can ensure that I have the subject in its right context. I try to make sure that I know more about the subject than I share or present so that I answer all the questions in my own mind before presenting any material publicly. It's been said that if there is a mist in the pulpit there is a cloud in the pews. Therefore, starting at the beginning and understanding the origins of a subject has a tendency to enhance the clarity of the presentation. For this reason, when I began to look at lessons learned from biblical characters I had to start with the first family of record. So I will begin this section with lessons learned from the first man, according to the biblical record – Adam.

In Part III of this book we look at creation and God's relationship with his creation, but for the purpose of the lessons learned, we will assume for now that the readers of this book believe that man and woman were created by God. The first man, Adam, provides for us several parenting lessons that I will uncover for you in this chapter. The Scriptures record that after everything that was necessary to sustain mankind was created, "The Lord God said, "It is not good for man to be alone. I will make a helper suitable for him." NIV (Genesis 2:18) …" Then the Lord God made a woman from the rib he had taken out of the man. The man said, "This is now bone of my bones and flesh of my flesh; she shall be called woman, for she was taken out of man." The Scripture goes on to say, "For this reason a man will leave his father and mother and be united to his wife, and they will become one flesh. The man and his wife were both naked, and they felt no shame." NIV (Genesis 2:22-25) This is the start of the story.

Adam and his wife, whom he named Eve, gave birth to their first two children after they were driven out of the place where God created them, as recorded in the third chapter of Genesis. They named their first son Cain and their second son they named Abel. It is clear from the biblical text that both Adam and Eve recognized that the Lord had given them children. In Genesis 4:1, Eve said, "... With the help of the Lord I have brought forth a man." NIV It goes on to say that later on she gave birth to his brother Abel. Over the course of time both Cain and Abel grew and took on their roles in the family structure and both had responsibilities and assignments; today we might call them chores. The Scripture says that Abel kept flocks, and Cain worked the soil. According to the biblical record, "In the course of time Cain brought some of the fruits of the soil as an offering to the Lord. But Abel brought fat portions from some of the firstborn of his flock." Where these two brothers learned about bringing offerings to the Lord, we are not told, but the only other people at this time as we know it were their parents, Adam and Eve; therefore, it would be safe to say that they learned this act of presenting offerings before the Lord from their parents if from anyone and most likely from Adam, their dad.

However, we are told that one brother's offering pleased God and one brother's did not please God. Cain's offering was displeasing to God, while Abel's offering was looked upon with favor. This angered Cain very much, even causing his face to become downcast. Now according to biblical record, the Lord had a conversation with Cain and asked him why he was angry and why was his face downcast. He also told Cain that there was an option and means by which he would be accepted. The text is clear when it says that Cain would be accepted, not his offering, but him. His offering represented who he was in his heart and the right offering meant he had the right heart. Abel's offering simply meant he had the right heart. He offered the best portion of the firstborn of his flock, which was viewed as the best that he had to give. Abel's offering also required the shedding of blood, which God always required by His own example with Adam and Eve for the forgiveness of sin. When Adam and Eve sinned, God sacrificed an animal to use its skin to cover them. In Genesis 3, Adam and Eve sewed fig leaves together to cover themselves following their disobedience to God's one prohibition. God replaced their fig leaves with a garment that He made for them from the animal's skin. So God made the first sacrifice by shedding the blood of an animal to cover Adam and Eve. Hebrews 9: 22 says that without the shedding of blood there is no remission of sins.

We know the rest of this story; we learned it in Sunday School. Cain lured his brother Abel out to the field and while they were in the field, Cain attacked his younger brother and killed him in the field. According to Scripture, God then returned to Cain for another conversation and He asked him, "Where is your brother Abel?" Cain replied, "I don't know." "Am I my brother's keeper?" The Lord said to Cain "What have you done? Listen! Your brother's blood cries out to me from the ground." Let me be perfectly clear when I say that every question God had asked Cain up to this point in both of their conversations was asked not to provide God with information that He did not know, but the questions were asked to give Cain an opportunity to come clean. God is so gracious He always provides us an opportunity to repent, which simply means to change our course of action and go in the direction of righteousness and righteous actions. When Cain failed to come clean, God's judgment was swift and certain. Cain was cursed and banished from the ground; that which he had previously been assigned to was no longer going to produce for him, and he would become a wanderer on the earth. One version of Scripture says he would become a vagabond. Cain was also marked for life less someone found him and killed him. Even in that, God alone reserved the right to enact vengeance. Dads, our kids, like Cain, are oftentimes fearful that the things they have done to others will be done to them.

Dads, I would like to pick up the lessons learned at this point now that we have the story of the first two sons. Let me begin with God's questions to Cain. God asked Cain five questions: NIV Genesis 4:6,9,10

1. Why are you angry?
2. Why is your face downcast?
3. If you do what is right, will you not be accepted?
4. Where is your brother?
5. What have you done?

Dads, the question of why Cain was angry is a question that we must ask our kids when we see that they are disposed to anger? Why are you angry? Cain's anger led him to destructive actions that culminated in him taking the life of his brother. Anger unharnessed is a dangerous weapon. That is one of the reasons that the Apostle Paul said, in Ephesians 6, for fathers not to provoke their children to anger, but grow them up in the nurture and admonition of the Lord. NIV

Why is your face downcast? Anger and the feeling of rejection can and often does show up symptomatically. Dads, just like God did with Cain, we have to recognize the symptoms of dysfunctional behaviors within our children and give them an opportunity to come clean with what is going on in their lives.

If you do what is right, will you not be accepted? This is about providing our children the opportunity to do the right thing. We should always give our children the chance to do what's right. In the business world we are taught to look for exceptions, to look for what was done wrong so it can be corrected. God says give your children the chance to do what's right then you don't have to correct them. I recall many years ago being assigned to an audit team that went to New Mexico to audit the Human Resources Department. It was one of my first trips for the company and one of the men who I had the utmost respect for was scheduled to receive our review of findings. When we arrived in New Mexico, the district personnel had pulled all the files that we were going to review and they had everything prepared for us to audit. I asked the HR manager, who headed up the team, why were we auditing files that they had already prepared for us. My thought was we would get a better picture if we randomly selected files to be audited. I never forgot his answer to my question. He said we don't conduct these audits necessarily to catch people doing things wrong; we conduct these audits to see that people can do the job right. Dads, we give our children the chance to do what's right; God gave Cain the chance to do the right thing. Are we better than God?

Where is your brother? What a powerful question? If we only asked this question more often, maybe then we wouldn't have so many brothers who have lost their way. Cain's reply to this question has permeated generation after generation. Are we our brother's keepers? I tell my kids, yes, you are your brother's and your sister's keeper. There is an expectation that our kids will look out after one another regardless of the circumstances.

The last question: "What have you done?" Many times our kids have done things that they know are wrong and we know they have done wrong; so the question is not to inform us, but it is to give them a chance to come clean and acknowledge what they have done. God knew what Cain did, He saw him when he did it and He could hear Abel's blood crying out from the ground. The intensity and magnitude of what Cain did was borne out in the fact that his brother's blood was literally screaming out from the grave. Although Cain could not hear his brother's blood, innocent blood that is shed is always heard by a just and infinitely holy God. Innocent blood always cries out for justice and vengeance to which only a holy and just God can fully enact. Up to this point in human history the ground had never tasted innocent blood accept the blood that was shed in sacrifice to its Creator. In Romans 8: 19-22 we learn that all of creation groans as it waits in eager anticipation of its liberation from the bondage of its own decay. What have you done is a powerful question that we ought to ask our kids when it is appropriate; it gives them the chance to come clean. However, even when and if our children come clean that does not shield them from the consequences of their actions. Cain did not come clean, but had he come clean there still would have been consequences for his actions because the wages for sin have always been and will continue to be death. There is always a price to be paid. God required that Cain pay a price for his sin and there was nothing that Adam could do about God's judgment; which leads me to my first lesson learned from Adam.

Dads, the lesson is never attempt to interfere with God's judgment.

Adam never tried to save his son from the judgment of God. Oftentimes, we want to intervene and soften the punishment of our children. We often think that we know what is best for our children when it comes to the discipline of God. Dads, when God puts His hands on your children you have to get out of the way and let God do what He alone knows is best for your children. You see, because Cain had tasted blood, what would have kept him from killing again? God knew that Cain needed to be banished to isolation so that he could experience the gravity of what he had done. Sometimes God must put our kids in positions of aloneness so that they comprehend the gravity of their actions. Like Adam, we should never attempt to interfere with the judgment of God in the lives of our children.

The second lesson learned is after suffering a loss move forward.

The Bible says that Cain moved forward and started a family, which, by the way, continued on in his unrighteous ways. It was out of his lineage that men began to take for themselves multiple wives. Adam and Eve, on the other hand, had another son whom they named Seth, and Eve said of Seth, "God has granted me another child in place of Abel, since Cain killed him." NIV Eve didn't forget, but she found a way to move forward. Often times after suffering a great loss, people get stuck and find it difficult, if not impossible, to move forward. I can't say I know what that feels like nor do I ever want to be able to say that I know that feeling, but I know that the continuation of life requires that we move forward. Adam and Eve moved forward by having more children and doing what God commanded them to do which was to be fruitful and multiply.

The third lesson learned is never give up on God.

I believe the Scriptures provide us with insight into how Adam and Eve were able to move forward. In the very next verse in Genesis 4:26 it says "...At that time men began to call on the name of the Lord." NIV Adam lived an additional 800 years after Eve gave birth to Seth, the replacement of Abel. So many times parents give up on God; Adam shows us that you can go on and God can and will bless your life if you just continue.

Lessons learned from the first family:

1. **In the midst of dysfunctionality we have to let God be God and not interfere with His discipline or judgment.**
2. **We don't give up on God; we continue to call upon the Lord in spite of the circumstances in which we find ourselves.**
3. **We have to keep living for the Lord in spite of the actions of our children.**

CHAPTER IX

Lessons Learned from Enoch — The Father of Methuselah (Genesis 5:18-25)

In the 40 years that I have been following and serving the Lord, I have no doubt listened to thousands of gospel messages and sermons from Genesis to the book of Revelation, but rarely have I heard a message or sermon about the man named Enoch. In fact, Scripture speaks of Enoch on only three occasions – Genesis 5, Hebrews 11, and Jude 14 – but Enoch teaches us a powerful lesson about being a dad. Enoch is first mentioned in Genesis 5, which sets the foundation for this discussion. In the single-chaptered book of Jude, verse 14 confirms for us that Enoch was the seventh from Adam. So Enoch provides us with lessons from antiquity. Genesis records that:

1. When Adam had lived 130 years and had a son named Seth, he lived another 800 years and had other sons and daughters, and he died after 930 years.
2. When Seth had lived 105 years and became the father of Enosh, he lived another 807 years and had other sons and daughters, and he died after 912 years.
3. When Enosh had lived 90 years and became the father of Kenan, he lived another 815 years and had other sons and daughters, and he died after 905 years.
4. When Kenan had lived 70 years and became the father of Mahalalel, he lived another 840 years and had other sons and daughters, and he died after 910 years.

5. When Mahalalel had lived 65 years and became the father of Jared, he lived another 830 years and had other sons and daughters, and he died after 895 years.
6. When Jared had lived 162 years and became the father of Enoch, he lived another 800 years and had other sons and daughters, and he died after 962 years.
7. "When Enoch had lived 65 years he became the father of Methuselah. And **after** he became the father of Methuselah, **Enoch walked with God 300 years** and had other sons and daughters. Altogether, Enoch lived 365 years. Enoch walked with God; then he was no more, because God took him away."

There are common themes that even the casual reader of the Bible discovers when reading the Genesis account of the early beginnings of humanity. The first three themes that I will point out are obvious. Mankind lived extended lifespans well into the hundreds of years. According to Genesis 1:26, because man was created in the image and likeness of God, he was created to live forever, but, unfortunately, sin interrupted God's original design and purpose for mankind, which we will explore in depth in part three of this book. However, even with the expanded lifespans, you will notice that man's longevity quickly began to decline. Later in time, the Psalmist declared in the Prayer of Moses in Psalm 90:10 that our lifespan would become four score and 10 years if we have the strength; that's seventy to eighty years, which is a far cry from 800 and 900 plus years. The second theme is that in antiquity men and women populated the earth, they had children and lots of them. A third theme is they all died with one exception, Enoch.

What was the distinguishing characteristic about Enoch that made him different from all the others who came before him? We know from Scripture that Adam and Eve walked in the cool of the garden in which they had been created and God spoke with them there in that garden. We also know, according to Genesis 4:26, that in the time of Seth men began to call on the name of the Lord. However, not all men called upon the name of the Lord. The family of Cain, who killed his brother Abel, built civilizations and they began the practices of polygamy in direct disobedience to God's command for a man to leave his mother and father and be joined to his wife and the two of them become one flesh. Nowhere in God's marriage order did He say or suggest that men should take multiple wives to help populate the earth. God's plan has always been and will continue to be one man and one woman. He does not change. He is the same today, yesterday and forever more. So what distinguished Enoch? Unlike Adam and Eve, who only heard God as they walked and the others who began to call upon the Lord, "Enoch walked with God." However, the careful reader will observe that Enoch's walk with God began "after" he became the father of Methuselah. One might wonder as I did, since Enoch walked with God, why God took him so soon in his life. He lived only 365 years when others were still living well into the hundreds of years. I think we find the answer to that question in Hebrews as the writer provides his commentary on the life of Enoch and others who are mentioned in that great list of heroes of faith. The writer said, "By faith Enoch was taken from this life, so that he did not experience death; he could not be found, because God had taken him away." NIV (Hebrews 11:5) There are a couple of observations I would make from what the writer said. First, Enoch's translation from this earth was predicated on his faith. Enoch demonstrated a faith in the eternal God that kept him walking with God for 300 years. He didn't just occasionally visit with God or follow after God from a distance; the idea implied is that Enoch had a consistent daily walk with God built on faith and trust in a redemptive process that only God could provide. Secondly, it appears that there was a search conducted for Enoch and he could not be found. Enoch was a man whose presence, though no doubt detestable, was missed when he was no more. I say detestable because of what is further said about him. The writer of Hebrews said that before Enoch was taken he was commended as one who pleased God. While Jude, on the other hand, said that Enoch prophesied of the coming judgment of God upon the men of his generation and called them ungodly sinners. Later in the book of Hebrews, the writer said of the men and women listed as heroes of faith: "...They went about in sheepskins and goatskins, destitute, persecuted and mistreated - the world was not worthy of them. They wandered in deserts and mountains, and in caves and holes in the ground. These were all commended for their faith." NIV (Hebrews 11:37-39)

Enoch was one of these types of men in his walk with God. It was not that Enoch walked with God in some vacuum or hiding out in some cave or out in the desert like many did, but Enoch walked with God while having the responsibility of a family. The Scripture says that he had other sons and daughters who were born after Methuselah, after he began walking with God. We often think that in order to have a committed relationship with God and to walk in holiness before Him that we have to live in isolation; Enoch proves that is not the case. Enoch walked with God in the midst of his people and his times. The birth of his son Methuselah expanded the sphere of his duties and his responsibilities increased to include the nurturing of a family. Enoch was faced with the tremendous challenge of raising a family in the midst of a generation in which every inclination of the thoughts of men's hearts was continually evil. Enoch prophesied of judgment against the world in which he had to raise his children. The judgment that he predicated was partially carried out in the time of his great grandson Noah when God flooded the earth and redeemed Noah and his family. The Scripture says that "The Lord saw how great man's wickedness on the earth had become, and that every inclination of the thoughts of his heart was only evil all the time." NIV (Genesis 6:5) It is in this environment that Enoch walked with God. I believe along with others that Enoch realized the severity of the human condition and he understood that in order for him to fulfill his responsibilities as a father to his children he had to walk with God. Dads, Enoch teaches us that it takes a relationship with God to properly manage the responsibilities that come with being a father in the midst of a wicked and perverse generation.

In 1880, Charles Henry Mackintosh, in his notes on the book of Genesis, "Things New and Old," wrote that much is involved in the three words "walked with God!"[6] According to Mackintosh, these three words involved: separation, self-denial, holiness, moral purity, grace, gentleness, humility, tenderness, zeal, energy, patience, long-suffering, faithfulness and an uncompromising decision! To walk with God means to comprehend everything within the realm of divine life, whether active or passive. Mackintosh said it involves the knowledge of God's character as He has revealed it. It too involves the intelligence of the relationship in which we stand to God. Mackintosh said it is not a mere living by rules and regulations; nor laying down plans of action; nor in resolutions to go here or there, to do this or that. To walk with God, he said, is more than any or all of these things. Furthermore, he said, walking with God will sometimes carry us right athwart (crossways) the thoughts of men, and even of our brothers, if they, too, are not walking with God. It may often bring against us the charge of doing too much; at other times, of doing too little; but it is that faith which enables one to "walk with God."[7]

One of the great dangers of men attempting to "walk with God" today is the subtle and not so subtle presence of compromise. In today's world, like in the world in which Mackintosh lived in the 1880s, there is a push to promote union or unity and if truth finds its way in that is fine too; instead of the promotion of truth and if union or unity is accomplished much the better for all concerned. Walking with God in a world characterized by compromise and tolerance takes a courage that few men and women possess. In today's world we treat compromise and tolerance like they are sacred. The destruction that followed the life of Methuselah, Enoch's first born son, was brought about because compromise and tolerance had gone astray. However, God was neither compromising nor was He tolerant. Now, He was patient with mankind, but not tolerant. God gave mankind the entire lifespan of Methuselah – 969 years – to change, and He gave mankind the visual confirmation for 100 years while Noah built the ark to change; that was patience not tolerance. His judgment on the earth, while gracious in that He saved Noah and his family, was not compromising. God has never been compromising nor has He ever been tolerant; gracious and long-suffering, but never compromising and tolerant of evil.

Enoch also teaches us that godly living has generational effects. Enoch was the father of Methuselah who lived 969 years. Methuselah is the oldest person of record in all of human history. I am reminded of Ephesians 6 where children are instructed to obey their parents in the Lord, and to honor their mother and father that it may go well with them and that they may enjoy long life on the earth. It's evident by God's response to Enoch's walk with Him that Enoch did some things right and not only did God bless him by taking him, but God also blessed his son, his grandsons and his great-grandsons and beyond. In fact, Enoch's line can be traced all the way to Joseph, who was the husband of Mary, the mother of Jesus whom he raised as his son. NIV (Luke 3:37)

Dads, our children ought to cause us, like Enoch, to walk with God. The fact that children bring with them the opportunity for us to be responsible for someone other than ourselves should be reason enough to cause us to walk with God. Our children look to us to show them what it means to have a relationship with God. Our children learn what it means to walk with God from us. The Scriptures are very clear when they use time markers such as: when, then, and after. These time markers let us know how things occurred and when things occurred; they provide us with a chronology of events. Enoch started to walk with God after he became Methuselah's father. Just as Methuselah was the impetus in Enoch's life, your children should be the driving force in your life. Our children should cause us fathers to want to know more about God so we can teach them. Our children should cause us to want to know more about God so we can model godly principles in their presence. Our children ought to cause us to want to have a better relationship with God so that they see and learn how their relationship can and should be. Our children ought to cause us to walk with God so that we are in close proximity to his blessings and, in fact, we become the benefactors of his blessings. Dads, if for no other reason, our children ought to cause us to walk with God so they can see and experience his love manifested through and toward us.

Lessons Learned from Enoch:

1. A relationship with God teaches you how to properly manage parental responsibilities.
2. A relationship with God has generational effects.
3. A relationship with God may cause you to stand alone in difficult circumstances.
4. A relationship with God may take you to places that you never imagined.
5. A relationship with God is not a temporary thing or condition.
6. A relationship with God means you welcome the Sovereign One to act with sovereignty in your life.
7. A relationship with God is to walk by faith.

CHAPTER X

Lessons Learned from Noah —
The Father of Nations

It is nothing short of ironic that we come to this tenth chapter and we are reflecting on the lessons learned from Noah, who was 10 generations removed from Adam, according to the biblical record. In the last chapter, we concluded by discussing Enoch and his walk with God. Regarding Enoch, I said it was after he became the father of Methuselah that he started his walk with God. I said that children matter and they ought to cause us to walk with God. Some might even say that children make us walk with God, but I would say that they ought to cause us to walk with God. I said that dads have an impact on their children's lives. In other words, when dads walk with the Lord, they have a transformative impact on the lives of their children for generations. Fathers may also and often do have a transformative impact on their children's lives when they don't walk with the Lord; which may and often does continue for generations. One is positive and one can be very negative but the transformation of impact is there none the same. Noah is a perfect example of the generational transformative consequences of a dad walking with God. Noah was 10 generations removed from Adam, but he was the great-grandson of Enoch and the grandson of his righteous grandfather, Methuselah.

Enoch influenced his great-grandson. In the midst of a perverse generation, Enoch lived a life that would impact his family for generations to come. Noah, like his great-grandfather, lived in a time of great wickedness. Genesis 6 records an environmental condition of spiritual and moral depravity in which Noah found himself living. The Scripture says:

> When men began to increase in number on the earth and daughters were born to them, the sons of God saw that the daughters of men were beautiful, and they married any of them they chose. Then the Lord said, "My Spirit will not contend with man forever, for he is mortal, his days will be a hundred and twenty years." The Nephilim were on the earth in those days – and also afterward – when the sons of God went to the daughters of men and had children by them. They were the heroes of old, men of renown. The Lord saw how great man's wickedness on the earth had become, and that every inclination of the thoughts of his heart was only evil all the time. The Lord was grieved that he had made man on the earth, and his heart was filled with pain. So the Lord said, "I will wipe mankind, whom I have created, from the face of the earth – men and animals, and creatures that move along the ground, and birds of the air – for I am grieved that I have made them." But Noah found favor in the eyes of the Lord.[8] NIV

The Scripture goes on to say that "Noah was a righteous man, blameless among the people of his time, and he walked with God." It is not surprising that the Bible uses the same phrase when describing Noah as it does when it describes his great-grandfather Enoch; they both walked with God. We don't know much about Noah's father, Lamech, because the Scripture chooses not to give us that record, but we do have the record of his grandfather and great-grandfather, both of whom were righteous men. Dads, our relationship with God, whether good or non-existent, has a generational transformative impact on the lives of our children. I could tell you story after story of sons and daughters who followed in the footsteps of their fathers and grandfathers. Stories of fathers or grandfathers who went into military service and their children also had military careers; stories of fathers who focused on higher education and their children and grandkids became educators or highly educated; unfortunate stories of dads who took not so positive routes and their children, likewise, followed in their footsteps. Dads, what you and I do matters because it has a generational impact on our children and our children's children.

So let me talk about Noah and how he demonstrated his character as a dad. In Genesis 6, God instructs Noah to begin the process of building an ark for himself, his family and the remnant of animals that God would preserve. God was very precise about the dimensions of the ark and the materials from which it was to be constructed. Furthermore, the Lord informed Noah that He was going to bring the floodwaters on the earth, but Noah, his family and the animal life that would enter the ark would be saved. The Bible says that "Noah did everything just as God commanded him." NIV (Genesis 6:22) Dads, this really is the key to our success as fathers and in life; we must do everything that God commands us to do as He commands us to do it. When we do all that God commands us to do, we protect our families and we preserve the life of our families. Dads, our obedience to the Lord is important to the success of our families. When others are being tolerant of the cultural norms and comprising their values, you and I have to stand firm and do what thus says the LORD. I often hear successful people talk about how firm their parents were, to that I say good. Their firmness, our firmness and willingness to take a firm stand in the midst of difficult circumstances is what develops character that our children want to emulate. Unfortunately, today we have too many dads who are giving ground and not standing firm.

Dads, sometimes, like Noah, you will have to labor in obscurity. How many dads do you know who work the graveyard shift, laboring in obscurity? From the time that Noah was born until he was 500 years old, he lived in apparent obscurity. It was when he was 500 years old that we are told he began to have children and he had three sons: Shem, Ham and Japheth. Now, I know that today's reader may find it difficult to comprehend people having children at this age, but it was not until Noah's lifetime as recorded in Genesis 6:3 that God pronounced the shortening of man's lifespan. So procreation up to that point appeared to have only been limited by one's lifespan, not by a biological clock as it were. So from the time we first learn of Noah becoming a father to the time that the rains began was 100 years. Noah labored in obscurity for 100 years. No doubt his contemporaries laughed at him and ridiculed him for building this monstrosity of an ark on land that had never experienced rain from heaven. The Scripture says that the earth had been watered by a mist that rose up from the earth and watered the surface of the ground. However, God had established a covenant with Noah, and God is not a man that He should lie; He said it was going to rain and rain it did. According to biblical record, "…all the springs of the great deep burst forth, and the floodgates of the heavens were opened. And rain fell on the earth forty days and forty nights." The Scripture reiterates the fact that before the rains began to fall, "Noah did all that the Lord commanded him." NIV (Genesis 7:5) Dads, imagine God telling you to do that which seems foolish, that which seems to make no sense; are you willing to do all that God commands you to do? If you read the biblical account of the flood you discover that God was very precise and extremely specific when it came to the details, and it was Noah's following of those detailed instructions that led to the preservation of not only his immediate family, but Noah's obedience's led to the preservation of nations and humanity.

Dads, we have to remember that our lives matter; how we live matters to our children for generations. Noah was 10 generations removed from Adam. The lessons that we learn from Noah is that, as dads, we have to do all that God commands us to do. Secondly, we learn that dads do what is required to provide protection for their children and family. The ark was the place of protection for Noah's family. I vividly recall my days in Columbus at Gospel

Tabernacle Church and how Bishop McCollum would often use the phrase "the ark of safety" when referencing what it meant to come to Christ. Like Noah and his family who entered the ark, believers enter into the body of Christ, which is in effect "the ark of safety," as Noah's ark was in his day. Third, we learn that dads provide for their families; that ark was the provision for Noah's family. Noah labored in obscurity; although all eyes were no doubt on Noah during those 100 years of building, the spotlight was really not on him. We dads have to remember that the spotlight doesn't have to be on us. If there is a spotlight, let it shine on those who we impact most – our children.

We learn two more critical lessons from Noah – patience and persistence. The Scripture says it rained for forty days and forty nights. However, the waters did not recede from the earth for another 150 days, and the ark rested on the mountains of Ararat. It was another three months before the tops of the mountains became visible. Then it was another forty days before Noah opened the window that he made in the ark to let a raven out to see if it could find food on dry ground; if any bird could find food, the raven could. After the raven, Noah sent a dove, but it could find no resting place for its feet, so Noah waited even longer and finally, after a year and two months, Noah and his family left the ark. The Scripture says that on the first day of the first month of Noah's six hundred and first year, the water had dried up from the earth and Noah removed the covering from the ark and saw that the surface of the ground was dry. Noah demonstrated for us great patience as he waited on God to complete his family's deliverance. Dads, sometimes we have to wait on God's deliverance. But, like Noah, while we wait, we have to do our part. Noah did his part; he opened the window, he sent out the raven, he sent out the dove on two occasions while he waited on God for further instructions. Noah demonstrated for us what it means to be persistent. His instruction came in verse 9: "Then God said to Noah, Come out of the ark, you and your wife and your sons and their wives. Bring out every kind of living creature that is with you – the birds, the animals, and all the creatures that move along the ground – so they can multiply on the earth and be fruitful and increase in number upon it." NIV (Genesis 8:15-17)

When Noah comes out of the ark, he teaches us a lesson that we dads should grab hold of and teach to our children: when God brings you through the storms in your life the first order of business is to praise and worship Him. Scripture says, "Then Noah built an altar to the Lord" and he offered the sacrifice of a burnt offering and when God smelled the aroma of his offering the Lord was pleased. The Lord then made a pledge to Noah that He would never again judge the earth in this manner and the seasons would never again be halted. To seal the covenant with Noah, God said, "I have set my rainbow in the clouds, and it will be the sign of the covenant between me and you and all living creatures of every kind." "...Never again will the waters become a flood to destroy all life. Whenever the rainbow appears in the clouds, I will see it and remember the everlasting covenant between God and all living creatures of every kind on the earth." NIV (Genesis 9:13,15,16)

Dads, Noah teaches us some great lessons which we will summarize, but, on a side note, God does not always deliver us from storms in the same way. In the last chapter, we observed that God delivered Enoch from the storm that was brewing by taking him unto Himself; thus Enoch was delivered from going through the storm. Noah, on the other hand, was delivered out of the storm. The same God who took Enoch is the same God who sent Noah through the storm, but delivered him out of it. I am so glad that God has provided dads like Noah and Enoch and many others as examples for us. They provide us with the template for how to be a godly dad, if we would just follow it. Noah's deliverance out of the storm provides us with tremendous hope for those times when we are in the storms of life. You see, Noah, just like the rest of mankind, was in the storm, but the difference was that Noah and his family were in the ark of safety. When you and I are in the storms of life, there is a place called "the ark of safety" and you will only find it in Jesus Christ and Him alone. Maybe you feel like I felt the day I recorded this chapter; the storms of life were all around me, pressures from every aspect of my life, but God has given me assurance that my family and I are in His ark of safety. Regardless of how hard the waves hit my proverbial boat and how high the waters rise, God says in the quietness of my heart "I got you covered!" If you recall, the ark had a covering and Noah didn't remove it until it was safe to do so by evidence of the dove returning with a freshly plucked olive leaf. In Scripture, the dove represents the spirit of peace and the olive represents forgiveness, which further demonstrates God's love and compassion for his children. God comforted Noah with the signs of peace in the dove and forgiveness with the olive leaf. We have that same comfort with the peace that the Holy Spirit gives us in the midst of life's storms and the forgiveness that Jesus Christ affords us when we put our faith in His finished work. Just like Noah we can have a firm footing in spite of the conditions that may exist all around us.

Dads, if you will believe the biblical record and grab hold of these lessons from Noah and do all that God tells you to do, like Noah, you will secure protection and provisions for your family. You may be called to labor in obscurity, you may have to wait with patience on the Lord, and you may have to be persistent, but know that God remembers. Genesis 8:1 says, "But God remembered Noah..." NIV and in 9:16 He again says, "...I will see it and remember..." NIV Dads, you are the difference makers in your family. You may not see it, you may not believe it, you may even be made to feel that neither you nor your presence matters in the family unit, but I want to assure you that dads matter. There is a billboard that I have recently seen around Southern California that says, "What can one person do? "Inspire someone! This question is positioned on the billboard opposite a picture of the late South African President Nelson Mandela, who became South Africa's first black president after spending 27 years imprisoned during that country's years of apartheid. What can one person do? Dads, one person in the hand of God can change the world; one person can certainly provide a model of success for his children and that person is you.

Lessons Learned from Noah:

1. Things that dads do have multi-generational transformative impact.
2. We dads must do all that God commands us to do.
3. Obedience to God protects your family through life's storms.
4. Labor in obscurity when necessary – God remembers your labor.
5. Be patient while waiting on God's deliverance for your family.
6. Be persistent while waiting on God's deliverance of your family.
7. Offer praise when God brings deliverance to your family.

CHAPTER XI

Lessons Learned from Abraham — The Father of the Faith

The Scripture says, "Abraham believed God, and it was credited to him as righteousness." NIV (Romans 4:3) If Abraham teaches us anything, he teaches us that, as dads, we must model faith and faithfulness before our family. Abraham has been called the father of the faith, not because he was the first patriarch to believe, but because his trial was the most personal and challenging of all his predecessors. At the end of the day he was asked to sacrifice his son of promise that God allowed him and Sarah to have. Although this was the ultimate test of faith, it was not the only test of his faith. Abraham had gone through a series of tests of his faith. The first test of his faith came after the death of his father, Terah, who died in the land of Haran when he was 205 years of age.

The Lord said to Abram before his name was changed to Abraham, "Leave your country, your people and your father's household and go to the land I will show you." NIV (Genesis 12:1) This first test was relatively easy, all Abram had to do was to leave; God would do the rest. His test came with seven promises attached to it:

1. Go to the land I will show you.
2. I will make you into a great nation.
3. I will bless you.
4. I will make your name great, and you will be a blessing.
5. I will bless those who bless you.
6. Whoever you curse I will curse.

7. All peoples on earth will be blessed through you.

Abram's job was easy, just leave. Unfortunately, today many who become fathers forget that they are supposed to leave to take on their responsibilities of becoming a dad. This first test of Abram's faith was met with success. The Scripture says, "So Abram left, as the Lord had told him." When Abram set out for the land of Canaan, the Promised Land, he built an altar and worshiped God; the altar solidified the test, it demonstrated that his faith was in God.

Abram's second test followed soon thereafter, but unfortunately he did not fare so well with his second test. The Scripture tells us that there was a famine in the land, so Abram went down to Egypt to live because the famine was severe. Egypt was not the place of God's provision as evidenced by that fact that Abram felt the need to conceal the truth about him and Sarah's true relationship as husband and wife. He chose rather to claim the aspect of their relationship that he thought would best protect their well being. God had given Abram these seven great promises, yet he did not believe that God could and would protect him and Sarah in Egypt. He feared the Egyptians would kill him and take Sarah because of her beauty, but if he and Sarah said they were brother and sister they would not kill him to take her, they would simply take her. While Abram and Sarah were half brother and sister, their marriage relationship superseded their sibling relationship. Abram failed test number two. Dads, Abram's failure teaches us that though we may fail, it does not make us failures; God can still use us when we return to Him in faith. Had Abram trusted God to provide for him and not gone down to Egypt he would have never found himself in the predicament in which he felt the need to mask the truth.

Abram's next test came when he returned to the Land of Promise after being put out of Egypt. This was a test of the heart. Would Abram separate from his nephew Lot in order to maintain peace in the family and among their servants? God had blessed Abram and Lot so much that the land could not support the size of their herds and Abram's herdsmen quarreled with Lot's herdsmen over the land. Abram told Lot less there be quarreling between my herdsmen and your herdsmen let us separate, you choose the land best suited for your herds. Lot looked upon the cities of Sodom and Gomorrah, and he pitched his tent near Sodom; Abram stayed in the Land of Promise. Abram once again successfully passed the test of faith in God. It was at that point when Abram was fully committed to being where God called him to be and doing what God called him to do that God said, "Lift up your eyes from where you are and look north and south, east and west. All the land that you see I will give to you and to your offspring forever. I will make your offspring like the dust of the earth, so that if anyone could count the dust, then your offspring could be counted. Go walk through the length and breadth of the land, for I am giving it to you." NIV (Genesis 13:14-17) Dads, until we do what God tells us to do we should not expect anything from the Lord. However, once we do what God says, there are no limits to what He will do for us.

Abram's courage was tested when Lot was captured along with the kings of Sodom and Gomorrah. Abram took about 320 trained men and pursued Lot's captors and rescued him from their hands. Abram's victory was so decisive that it led to another test of his faith. Would he take money for his victory or would he give God the glory for the victory? Once again Abram passed the test and refused to accept money for what God had done through him; less someone say that they made Abram rich, when, in fact, God's hand of blessing on Abram's life made him a wealthy man. Dads, when put in difficult situations we must be courageous enough to take action and wise enough to know when to say no.

Earlier I said that failing doesn't mean that we are failures. The Word of God does not leave out the failures of the biblical characters and thank God it does not. Abram failed terribly when it came to fatherhood. God promised him and Sarah that He would give them a son in their old age. You would think that with their history with God, Abram and Sarah would have trusted God to do the miraculous and give them a child. They were just a few generations away from men and women having children well into their hundreds. The last biblical character that we looked at was Noah and he had children at 500 years old. However, after the flood, God declared the shortening of the lifespan of mankind, so it's understandable that for Abram and Sarah to conceive at their age would be unnatural. It is conceivable from their responses that Abram actually believed God; it's pretty evident that Sarah did not. The fact that Sarah took matters into her own hands demonstrates her lack of faith in the promise of God. Dads, when we take things that God is in control of into our own hands we will always make a mess of things, because His ways are not our ways and His thoughts are so much higher than our thoughts. He sees things before they happen and we see only in the present. God sees the past, the present, the future present and the future. You may ask "What is the future present?" The future present are those things that will happen in the future, but God speaks of them in the present as though they have already happened because they are certain because of His declaration of them. When we take matters into our own hands we are operating with limited knowledge of the outcome, whereas God knows the outcome before the beginning.

When Sarah took things into her own hands, she provided Abram with a woman of convenience who produced a child of chance. Abram's child of chance would be one, if not the greatest, of his failings, but the grace of God kept him from becoming a failure. God did not hide Abram's failure, and Hagar, the Egyptian maidservant, never let either him or Sarah forget it. The Scripture says that once Hagar realized she was pregnant, she began to despise Sarah. There was bad blood between Hagar and Sarah, and Abram was caught in the middle between his wife and the woman who was having his child. How many times have we seen this story turn out good? However, God, through His grace and mercy, worked the situation out to His glory. When Hagar could no longer take the abuse from Sarah, she ran away, but God found her and the angel of the Lord sent her back to her mistress. The angel also told her that God would remember her son and would increase her descendants like those of Abram and Sarah. However, her son would be characterized as a wild donkey of a man; his hand would be against everyone and everyone's hand against him, and he would live in hostility toward all his brothers. Dads, this just goes to show you that when we, like Abram, fail to trust God to do what he says he would do and we take matters into our own hands we never know how things will end up. The Scripture says that all good and perfect gifts come from the Lord. Ishmael was a child of chance while Isaac was a child of promise.

Thank God that his capacity to extend grace supersedes our failures. When Abram was 99 years old, 13 years after the birth of Ishmael, the Bible says the Lord appeared to Abram and identified Himself and said, "I am God Almighty, walk before me and be blameless." What God was saying to Abram in the name that He used to reveal Himself (El-Shaddai which means God Almighty) was twofold. One, God (El, "the mighty One" and Shaddai, "all-powerful," hence "all-sufficient") was saying He is able to meet the most humanly hopeless and most desperate needs of His people.[9] God was saying you may have failed me, but I will never fail you. Two, He went on to seal his confidence in Abram's ability to become what he was born to be by reasserting His promise to him. Dads, you and I might not be all that we were born to be, but if we put our trust in the Lord, we can become all that He designed us to be.

God reaffirmed with Abram what theologians refer to as "The Abrahamic Covenant." However, in order for Abram to become what God had designed him to be, Abram had to become Abraham. God designed Abram to be Abraham, that is, "the father of many nations." Dads, most often when God has plans for our lives and He does, He has to change us from what we use to be to what He desires us to become. Abram needed to be changed from a father to a father of nations. However, great responsibilities most often require great faith, which is cultivated by great trials. James 1:2 says, "Consider it pure joy, my brothers, whenever you face trials of many kinds, because you know that the testing of your faith develops perseverance. Perseverance must finish its work so that you may be mature and complete, not lacking anything." NIV James 1:12 says, "Blessed is the man who perseveres under trial, because when he has stood the test, he will receive the crown of life that God has promised to those who love him." NIV Dads, when God wants to entrust us with great responsibilities, they are most often preceded by times of great testing.

Abraham's greatest test was yet before him. Leaving his father's country and the ramifications there of was nothing compared to the test that was yet to come. The test that required Abram to send Hagar and Ishmael off on their own, while difficult, pales in comparison to the test that was yet in front of him. These were mere precursors to his final test of faith. The Bible says that, "Some time later God tested Abraham." We know the story from Sunday School and Vacation Bible Study or youth retreats; it is the story that defines who Abraham became. God instructed Abraham to go to Mount Moriah and offer his son; the son of promise as a burnt offering. The burnt offering in the Levitical Offering system was the sacrificial offering of a specific type of spotless animal as a substitute for the one presenting the offering. The presenter would place his hand on the head of the animal which signified his connection with the animal. The burnt offering was also the only offering that was completely consumed on the altar and none was left for the priest or anyone else. The offering was fully consumed by the fire before the Lord and it was to Him a sweet aroma. That is what God instructed Abraham to make of his son. Really, God was asking him to do two things: first, give your son, the one I gave you by way of a promise, give him, that son, back to me; secondly, God was asking Abraham to make it a complete commitment, as the burnt offering was always fully consumed by the fire upon which it lay.

If this were the end of the story, it would be a horrible outcome; God promised Abraham this son and gave him this son in his old age only to turn around and demand that he sacrifice him to demonstrate his faith. However, the story didn't end there for Abraham, and our story may not end where we think it ends. God demonstrated to Abraham that He can provide a ram in the bush at the right time for the right occasion, and He will do the same for us. The ram showing up in the bush at the right time in the right place was never the question; the question was and is always will we do what He tells us to do? If we do what God tells us to do, the ram is His responsibility not ours. Dads, our responsibility is to do what He tells us to do and let Him be responsible for the results. God told Abraham where to go and what to do when he got there and that was all Abraham was responsible for doing. What Abraham didn't know about the place that God told him to go was what the place meant to God. God told Abraham to go to Mount Moriah, which means the place where God will provide. Dads, you and I must always be sensitive to the fact that where God leads us, He assumes the responsibility for ensuring that we have the provisions required.

Like Abraham did in his final test of his faith, we must trust fully in what God has promised. The angel of the Lord declared to Abraham when God stayed his hand and prevented him from sacrificing his son: "Do not do anything to him, now I know that you fear God, because you have not withheld from me your son, your only son." NIV That is the son of promise. James 2:23 says, "Abraham believed God, and it was credited to him as righteousness," and he was called God's friend. NIV

Lessons Learned from Abraham:

1. **Failing does not make you a failure.**
2. **Until we do what God says we should not expect anything from Him.**
3. **It takes courage to act in faith in difficult situations.**
4. **When we take things into our own hands we make a mess of them.**

5. **When we trust in God we become who He designed us to be.**
6. **God will not entrust us with great responsibilities prior to great trials.**
7. **Our responsibility is to do what God tells us to do and let Him be responsible for the results.**

CHAPTER XII

Lessons Learned from Jacob — The Father of Many Nations

When I started writing this book I ask myself the question: Was there a thematic Scripture verse that would easily define the message I am trying to get across to dads and those who would be dads? As I was studying the life of Abraham, it dawned on me that being a dad was really about taking all that you have and depositing it into the lives of your children, which is what I have tried to do over these last 30 years of raising my children. Along the way, I came across an obscure passage about Abraham in Genesis 25 that really defines what it means to be a dad. Verse 5 says, "Abraham left **everything** he owned to Isaac." NIV In other words, everything he owned belonged to his children. Jacob, like his grandfather, also had one defining aspect of his parenting; unfortunately, it ripped his family apart and caused them to become extremely dysfunctional. The Scripture records how Jacob parented in two verses of Genesis 37: 3-4, where it says, "Now Israel (Jacob) loved Joseph more than any of his other sons, because he had been born to him in his old age; and he made a richly ornamented robe for him. When his brothers saw that their father loved him more than any of them, they hated him and could not speak a kind word to him." NIV

Favoritism is probably one of the most dangerous behaviors parents can engage in with their children. Like many families today, Jacob was raising a blended family. Jacob had worked seven years for his uncle Laban for his daughter Rachel's hand in marriage, but his uncle deceived him into marrying her sister Leah first. Jacob and

Leah had six sons together: Reuben, Simeon, Levi, Judah, Issachar and Zebulun. Jacob had no love for Leah, but her father tricked him into the marriage because she was the older of two sisters. Jacob also had two sons by Leah's maidservant: Gad and Asher. After working another seven years for Rachel, whom he loved, they married, but Rachel was barren and could not have children. So she gave Jacob her maidservant, and they had two sons: Dan and Naphtali. Over time Rachel's jealousy grew against her sister and she began to cry out to the Lord and He remembered her and the Scripture says that He listened to her and opened her womb and she gave birth to two sons: Joseph and Benjamin. Rachel died giving birth to Benjamin. These twelve sons of Jacob became the Nation of Israel of whom Jacob is the father.

Dads, Jacob's favoritism toward his son Joseph wreaked havoc in his family and favoritism will wreak havoc in your family as well. I don't have one child who is more special than the others or more attractive than the others or more of anything than the others so I don't know and never want to know how that feels, but what I do have is insight into the outcome of favoritism as seen through the life of Jacob. Favoritism, brought about jealousy, which led to deceit, that led to murderous actions, that led to more deceit; it led to enslavement and imprisonment, it led to false accusations being lodged and much more. Nothing good comes out of favoring one child over another, yet so many parents find themselves caught in this trap.. The gifted child is favored over the not so gifted child. The athletic child is favored over the athletically challenged child. The biological child is favored over the step-child. Like Jacob, the child of your old age is favored over the children of your youth. Given time we could probably name a hundred different scenarios in which we find ourselves favoring one child over another, but it is one of the most detrimental behaviors you and I as dads could ever do to our families.

Jacob's practice of favoritism showed up when he gave Joseph a special robe. Joseph no doubt paraded around in front of his brothers and they hated him because of it. To top it off, God showed Joseph a dream that he would one day rule over his brothers and the entire family of Israel and they would someday bow before him. Imagine your younger children telling the older children that someday they are going to work for them and serve them. What do you think would happen in your house today? I suspect that our kids would not be so pleased to hear that kind of talk either. The Bible says that Joseph's brothers became jealous of him, but his father Jacob kept the matter in mind. Joseph's brothers laughed at him and called him a dreamer and they even plotted and attempted to kill him. However, his older brother, Reuben, stood up to the other brothers and said let's not kill him, but let's throw him into a pit in the desert. Another brother, Judah, came up with the bright idea to sell Joseph into slavery because there was no profit in keeping him in a pit, so they sold him to a passing Midianite caravan of merchants. Dads, this brought out another characteristic in the brothers – greed. God forbid they should shed their brother's blood, but selling him for profit was acceptable to them. This was a dysfunctional family.

Most of you know how the story unfolded; Joseph ended up in Egypt as a servant to a man named Potiphar, who was an Egyptian official who served as the captain of the guard for Pharaoh the King of Egypt. Joseph became very successful in all that he did and was promoted to the highest level in his master's house. Not only did the Lord bless Joseph, but his blessings were upon everything that Potiphar had as well. Joseph was in charge of everything until the day Potiphar's wife falsely accused him of trying to seduce her, when, in fact, she was the one who tried to seduce him. Her false accusation led to Joseph's imprisonment for more than two years. Dads, one can easily make the connection between Jacob's dysfunctional behaviors toward his children and Joseph's predicament in Egypt. Favoritism is a dysfunctional behavior and should never be practiced in a family.

Dads, even in bad and dysfunctional family situations, God is never dysfunctional; He always has everything in control. Although Joseph was imprisoned, God was able to use him to interpret the dreams of his cellmates, the butcher and the baker. This eventually led to him interpreting dreams for the Pharaoh. Through God's providence He allowed Joseph to be exalted to the number two official in all of Egypt. God used Joseph to prepare the people and the land for a famine that was on the horizon. Thirteen years had passed since Joseph's brothers sold him into slavery and lied to their father Jacob and told him that he had been attacked by a wild animal and killed. Joseph had gone from being a boy hated by his older brothers to becoming the man who would save not only their lives, but the lives of their entire nation. These same brothers who lied to their father about Joseph's fate also lied to Joseph upon meeting him in Egypt, although they did not recognize him but he recognized them. They said, "Your servants are honest men…" NIV (Genesis 42:10) Favoritism made liars out of Jacob's sons.

When Joseph could no longer stand keeping his identity secret from his brothers who had come to Egypt to buy food for their father's house, he let them know that he was their brother, the one that they sold into slavery. Joseph gives us insight into how God can take that which is dysfunctional and turn it into a blessing. In Genesis 45:4,5, the account of Joseph and his brothers reunion says that when Joseph could no longer control himself, he cried out with a loud cry and wept before all his attendants. He said to his brothers, "I am your brother, Joseph, the one you sold into Egypt! And now, do not be distressed and do not be angry with yourselves for selling me here, because it was to save lives that God sent me ahead of you." NIV God took their dysfunction and used it to save His people. When Jacob finally learned that his son was not dead, he joined him in Egypt and was given the fertile land of Goshen for all his flocks and herds.

After Jacob arrived in Egypt and saw his son for the first time in over thirteen years, he was presented to Pharaoh and Jacob blessed him. The Pharaoh asked Jacob his age and Jacob's response gives us great insight into his life. Jacob told Pharaoh, "The years of my pilgrimage are a hundred and thirty. My years have been few and difficult, and they do not equal the years of the pilgrimage of my fathers." NIV (Genesis 47:9) Jacob shows us what dysfunctional parenting does to a family and to a life. Two of Jacob's sons, Simeon and Levi, slaughtered an entire town of men after one man violated their sister; Reuben slept with his father's concubine; Issachar was strong, but lazy; Dan introduced idolatry into Israel; and Benjamin, the youngest son, was a ravenous wolf. The actions of Jacob's sons can be attributed right back to Jacob's practice of favoritism.

After Jacob's death in Egypt, his sons approached Joseph because they thought surely he would treat them like they had treated him now that their father was gone. However, Joseph showed once again that God takes dysfunction and makes it functional. When the brothers came to make their case to him for mercy; the Scripture records Joseph's response: "But Joseph said to them, "Don't be afraid. Am I in the place of God? You intended to harm me, but God intended it for good to accomplish what is now being done, the saving of many lives." NIV (Genesis 50:19-20). How many times have I said this, how many times has God taken a bad situation and turned it into a good thing for His glory? No one wants to be thrown into a pit; no one wants to be taken advantage of and abused; and God forbid that anyone is sold into servitude. The fact is, God can take any situation, no matter how hopeless it may appear, and turn it to His glory. Jacob's life as a dad is seen in the dysfunctional behavior he exhibited and the dysfunctional behavior that his sons exhibited; yet God used him to be the father of many nations through his twelve sons.

Lessons Learned from Jacob:

1. **Favoritism is dysfunctional behavior and should never be practiced in a family.**
2. **Favoritism produces destructive family behaviors:**
   a. **Jealousy**
   b. **Deceitfulness**
   c. **Murderous actions**
   d. **Enslavement**
   e. **Imprisonment**

   f. **False Accusations**
   g. **Greed**

3. **Favoritism made dishonest men of Jacob's sons.**
4. **God can turn our dysfunctional parenting around for His glory.**
5. **God grants favor without practicing the destructiveness of favoritism.**

CHAPTER XIII

Lessons Learned from Eli the Priest —
When judgment strikes in the house of God

How many times have you and I heard it said that "Christians" are worse sinners than the people in the clubs on Friday and Saturday nights? Or how many times have you heard people talk about "PK's" (preacher's kids) and how they live unrighteous lives. Unfortunately, some of what people say may prove to be true, as was the case with Eli, the priest of Israel, and his two sons, Hophni and Phinehas. This story of a father, who was a spiritual leader, and his sons has always been special to me, largely due to their outcome. As my own son was growing up in the church, I was well aware of the danger of him behaving like a Hophni or a Phinehas, because we brought him up around the things of God. The concern was always that because we brought our kids up around the things of God, they may assume a relationship with God when, in fact, maybe they did not have one. As a result, their actions would not reflect their assumptions, but rather a reality that maybe they did not know God. It is dangerous for us to assume that because we know God our children know God and will act accordingly. Eli knew God and had a relationship with God and served God. However, his sons neither knew God nor did they serve God, but they held positions in the tabernacle as though they had a relationship with God. The Scripture says in 1 Samuel 1:3 that year after year men went up to Shiloh to worship the Lord Almighty, and the two sons of Eli, Hophni and Phinehas, were priests of the Lord. However 1 Samuel 2:12

says, "Eli's sons were wicked men; they had no regard for the Lord." NIV

The Hophni and Phinehas effect is seen all too often in the church today. Kids grow up around the teachings of God and we adults assume because they are around all the time they actually have a growing relationship with the Lord. Hophni and Phinehas were priests because they were born into the ancestry of Aaron, who was the brother of Moses of whom the Lord had declared would serve in the priesthood. (Genesis 28 and 29) They had no relationship with the Lord. They simply did like many today, they went through the motions. However, they had no regard for the Lord or the things of the Lord, or his people. Hophni and Phinehas had a dad who was doing the work of the Lord by serving as the priest in the tabernacle at Shiloh. It was to Shiloh that Hannah and her husband Elkanah went year after year and brought their offerings and it was there that Hannah prayed for a son. It was at Shiloh that Eli pronounced a blessing on Hannah and the Lord blessed her and she gave birth to a son and named him Samuel.

Samuel's mother Hannah made a vow to the Lord that if He gave her a son she would give that son back to the Lord for a life of service. The Bible says that the Lord remembered Hannah and he blessed her with a son. After Hannah completed the Hebrew tradition of weaning her son, she and her husband took the boy back to Shiloh and presented him to Eli to be raised in the tabernacle before the Lord. Dads, there are two notes that I want you to observe: first, Hannah's husband Elkanah did not interfere with the vow she made, in fact, according to the Scriptures, Elkanah told Hannah, "Do what seems best to you..." NIV (1 Samuel 1:23) Secondly, Samuel was brought to Eli so that he could learn how to serve the Lord. Dads, sometimes you and I have to get out of the way and let God do with our children what He has planned for them.

Samuel grew up in the service of the Lord alongside Eli's sons, yet their relationship with God could not have been more different. Samuel grew up learning to listen to and for the voice of God, while Eli's sons ignored the voice of God and disregarded the things of

God. The story goes that Samuel, while in the care of Eli, hears the voice of God calling him, but presuming that it is Eli he goes to him on three occasions on the same night to respond to the call of his name and three times Eli says I did not call you. However, the third time Samuel goes to Eli, the Scripture says Eli realized that the Lord was calling the boy. So Eli tells Samuel if he calls you again respond by saying "Speak, Lord, for your servant is listening." The Bible says, "The Lord came and stood there, calling as at the other times, 'Samuel! Samuel!' Then Samuel said, 'Speak, for your servant is listening.'" NIV (1 Samuel 3:8-10) Little did Samuel know that God had come to the end of the line with Hophni, Phinehas and Eli.

While Eli was charged with raising Samuel to serve the Lord, he had failed to discipline his own sons for their disregard for the Lord and the things of God. Earlier, I said that oftentimes our children just go through the motions; going through the motions when it comes to matters pertaining to the Lord can be and often proves detrimental. The priests, according to Leviticus 7:34-35, were allotted a portion of the offerings for their sustenance after the offering was presented to the Lord. God was never to receive what was left over or remaining after everyone else got his share; God was always to receive the offering first. It's no different today. God should receive the first fruits of our labor, not what's left over after others have received their portion. That is the divine order of blessing. However, the Scripture records that Hophni and Phinehas would take their portion first, by force if necessary, before it had been offered to the Lord. The Bible says, "This sin of the young men was very great in the Lord's sight, for they were treating the Lord's offering with contempt. But Samuel was ministering before the Lord." NIV (1 Samuel 2:17-18a)

What made their sin even more grievous was the fact that not only did they steal from God, but they also added sexual promiscuity. The Scripture says that Hophni and Phinehas took the women who served at the entrance of the tabernacle and slept with them. So there were two charges against Eli's sons: they stole that which belonged to the Lord, and they were sexually promiscuous in the house of

God. The Scripture states clearly that Eli heard about everything his sons were doing and he attempted to address it with them, however, they refused to listen to their dad's rebuke. I recall years ago having a conversation with a friend who had recently become a dad and he said the one thing that he dreaded was the day that his son would no longer have a reverential fear of him. I clearly understood what he was saying because I, too, had the same concern. My friend was saying that he never wanted there to come a time when he could not garner his son's respect so that when he, as dad, said something his son wouldn't listen. Hophni and Phinehas had stopped listening to their dad. Their disregard for discipline had grown from one stage to the next; they disregarded their vocation; they disregarded the things of God; they disregarded the people of God and they disregarded God Himself and their dad. Often times when things get so far off course and God decides to intervene, his judgment is irrevocable, as was the case with the family of Eli.

In all of my studies of the Scripture, one of the things that I've learned over the years is that when God is going to take action against his chosen servants he always lets them know in advance. It is never a surprise when God decides to act. While time does not permit me to review case by case, a cursory study of Scripture reveals this pattern. The classic example is when God spoke to Moses and charged him with the responsibility of delivering the children of Israel out of Egypt. Moses was given specific instructions to go before the Pharaoh and bring God's people out of Egypt. God also revealed to Moses what he would do to Pharaoh to cause him to release the children of Israel. Exodus 6:1 reads: Then the Lord said to Moses, "Now you will see what I will do to Pharaoh: Because of my mighty hand he will let them go; because of my mighty hand he will drive them out of his country." NIV

The case of God's judgment against Eli's house was no different. The Bible says a man of God came to Eli and told him, this is what the Lord says: "Did I not clearly reveal myself to your father's house when they were in Egypt under Pharaoh? I chose your father out of all the tribes of Israel to be my priest, to go up to my altar, to burn incense, and to wear an ephod in my presence. I also gave your father's house all the offerings made with fire by the Israelites. Why do you scorn my sacrifice and offering that I prescribed for my dwelling? Why do you honor your sons more than me by fattening yourselves on the choice parts of every offering made by my people Israel." NIV (1 Samuel 2: 27b – 29) The first thing that God does with Eli is to lay out his case against him so that there is no surprise. Eli knew exactly why God's hand of judgment was coming upon him. God's judgment upon Eli would be twofold: first, there would not be another old man in the family line of Eli. Could it be that because Eli's sin occurred in his old age that God decided that old age would never again come to his family line? Secondly, God's judgment was that Eli's sons, Hophni and Phinehas, would both die on the same day.

Not only did the Lord send a man of God to inform Eli of his irrevocable judgment, but he also revealed his judgment to Samuel. Remember earlier I said that God had called Samuel in the night and Eli instructed Samuel to respond by saying, "Speak, for your servant is listening." When he did, the Lord said to Samuel, "See I am about to do something in Israel that will make the ears of everyone who hears of it tingle. At that time I will carry out against Eli everything I spoke against his family, from beginning to end. For I told him that I would judge his family forever because of the sin he knew about; his sons made themselves contemptible and he failed to restrain them. Therefore, I swore to the house of Eli, the guilt of Eli's house will never be atoned for by sacrifice or offering." NIV (1 Samuel 3:11-14) When Samuel revealed to Eli all that the Lord had spoken to him, Eli said in response, "He is the Lord; let him do what is good in his eyes." NIV (1 Samuel 3:18)

As the narrative continues to unfold, the Israelites at that time went out to fight against the Philistines, and they were sorely defeated and lost some four thousand men on the battlefield. Dismayed at how God could allow such a thing to occur, the people of God decided to go back into battle, but this time they would take the ark of the covenant of the Lord Almighty with them into battle. Once again, they were sorely defeated, only this time they lost thirty thousand foot soldiers and the ark of God was captured, and Eli's sons were both killed that day. I often tell people that God's perspective of life and death is much different than ours. Thirty four thousand Israelites died in that battle, but within that same battle, God's judgment was upon two specific men – Hophni and Phinehas. Upon hearing of the death of his sons and the capturing of the ark of God, Eli, who was old and heavy, fell backward off his chair and broke his neck and died as well. Upon hearing of the death of her husband and father-in-law, Phinehas' wife who was pregnant at the time went into labor and gave birth to a son and named him Ichabod, which means "The glory has departed from Israel" because of the capture of the ark of God and the deaths of her father-in-law and her husband.NIV (1 Samuel 4:21)

This story of Eli and his two sons is a tragic story, but it lets us know that God does not leave out the bad because it is embarrassing or somehow hurtful to his name or his reputation; he includes it along with the good so that we can learn from history. As my wife and I were raising our children, I would often tell our son, in particular, that I was not going to be an Eli. In other words, I would not sit by and let him live a life of destructive behavior and not address it in a serious way. So when it came to areas of discipline, particularly as it related to the things of God and the person of God, there was little room for tolerance. I realize that in today's society to say that you are intolerant is taboo, but, as for me and my house, I was not going to be an Eli. So let me make some observations from the parenting of Eli:

1. Eli failed to ensure that while his sons were around the things of God, they developed a relationship with God. (1 Samuel 1:3; 2:12)
2. Eli honored his sons more than he honored God. (1 Samuel 2:29)

3. Hophni and Phinehas scorned the Lord's prescribed sacrifice. (1 Samuel 2:29a)
4. Eli participated in his sons' wickedness by eating what they brought home even though he had heard about how they were taking the best parts for themselves, by force if necessary. (1 Samuel 2:23, 29; 4:18)
5. God's judgment upon Eli's house was irrevocable. (1 Samuel 2:30-34)
6. God's judgment was swift. (1 Samuel 2:34; 4:11)
7. God never surprises us with his judgment. (1 Samuel 2:30-34; 3:11-14)

My observations lead me to the lessons learned from the life of Eli:

1. **Dads, sometimes when we attempt to afford our children the best that life has to offer, we fail to make them better.**
2. **If we allow our children to disregard God, what will prevent them from disregarding others, us included?**
3. **Never participate in your children's wrong doing; your participation condones their actions.**
4. **Dads, some things require more than a verbal rebuke, they require clear and specific actions be taken to express your disapproval and intolerance of your children's conduct.**
5. **How we fathers respond to the conduct of our children can and often does have devastating long-term consequences.**
6. **God requires our first and our best be given to him, and he will ensure that we have all that we need.**
7. **Dads, we must allow God to do what is good in his eyes when it comes to our children's lives as well as our own.**

CHAPTER XIV

Lessons Learned from Job —
The Father of Integrity

People of every generation have asked the question: "Why do the innocent suffer?" How many times have you and I heard it said if God was such a loving being how could he allow the innocent to suffer? The story of Job is a story of human suffering and divine justice. In the realm of theology it is commonly call theodicy (from the Greek words "Theos" which means God and "dike" which means justice.) Job's experience with theodicy, like many of us, was an experience in which he knew too little about God's justice to understand. Oftentimes, we have too little knowledge of what God is doing behind the curtain, as it were, to understand our present reality. As a result of our general deficiencies in our depth of knowledge about God, we often make the mistake of blaming God for suffering, and we conclude that he is somehow unjust in his treatment of the innocent. I work in a region of the country in which there could and often is some type of natural disaster occurring every day; from earthquakes and firestorms out west, to hurricanes and tornados in the southwest and floods and snow storms in the Midwest. Just the weather alone and the inherent devastation that it leaves behind is enough to ask the question of theodicy: "Why do the innocent suffer?"

Before we dive into the lessons learned from Job's life, there is a short story in the New Testament Book of John in chapter nine of a man who was born blind. The story is that Jesus had been at the place called the Mount of Olives and he was in discourse with the teachers of the Jewish law and a group called the Pharisees and at the end of his discourse they attempted to stone him for declaring that before Abraham was born, "I Am." However, because it was neither the time nor the method by which Jesus was sent here to die, he escaped their attempt to stone him and he came across a man who was blind from birth. As he came to the man, his disciples asked him, "Rabbi, who sinned, this man or his parents, that he was born blind?" In the disciples' question is this idea of theodicy, something must have happened or someone must have done something to cause the man to be born blind. Suffering must be the result of some wrongdoing. Job's friends were convinced and they let him know that his suffering had to be the result of him or his children doing something wrong for which God was punishing him. Job's friends, like many of us oftentimes, lacked the spiritual insight into the divine will of God for our lives and the higher purpose for the things that occur in our lives. Let's go back to the story of the blind man and the answer to the disciples' question: Who did sin, this man or his parents? "Neither this man nor his parents sinned," Jesus said, "but this happened so that the work of God might be displayed in his life." NIV (John 9:3) The story of Job teaches us that sometimes God has higher purposes of which we do not have knowledge.

Theodicy
God's Justice

Dads, I want us to take a look at a man who by all outward appearances would be considered a very successful man in his time and even in today's economy. Bible readers are introduced to Job in the first chapter of the book that bears his name and we are provided with a description of his character, his family, his wealth, his status in the community, his family's lifestyle and his religious practices. Regarding Job's character, we are told three things:

1. He was blameless and upright.
2. He feared God.
3. He stayed away from evil.

Regarding his family, Job had seven sons and three daughters and one wife. As it relates to his possessions, Job had the following:

- 7,000 sheep
- 3,000 camels
- 500 yoke of oxen
- 500 donkeys
- A large number of servants

Regarding Job's status in the community, the Scripture records that "He was the greatest man among all people of the East." NIV (Job 1:3)

Regarding his family's lifestyle, Job's seven sons would take turns having feast at their homes and would invite the three sisters and they would eat and drink together on a regular basis.

The Meeting in Heaven– Job 1:6-22

Regarding Job's religious practices, after every feast that his children would have Job would send someone, most likely the priest, and have his children purified. The Bible says that early in the morning Job would sacrifice a burnt offering for each of them thinking, "Perhaps my children have sinned and cursed God in their hearts." This was Job's regular custom. As the dad, Job was always mindful of his children's potential for being out of step with God, and he took precautionary measures to ensure that God's requirements were fulfilled.

While Job practiced his customary acts of righteousness, little did he know that a divine meeting had taken place of which he was the topic of discussion. How often has a closed door meeting taken place and, unbeknown to you or I, we were the topic of discussion? Job was the topic of just such a meeting that Scripture says changed his life forever. The story of Job is a tragic one for which only God can properly respond, however, in the midst of Job's tragedy, we, as dads, learn how to be righteous fathers in the midst of tremendous loss.

The Scripture says, "One day the angels came to present themselves before the Lord, and Satan also came with them." The Lord asked Satan, "Where have you come from?" Satan's reply was descriptive of what he does even to this day. He said, "From roaming through the earth and going back and forth in it." NIV The idea within Satan's reply is that he had been searching the earth to see if there really was someone who was living up to the standard set by God; the standard that he himself did not live up to which resulted in him being cast from heaven, as detailed in Isaiah 14:12-17. In this heavenly meeting of the angels before the throne of God, the Lord asked Satan, "Have you considered my servant Job?" Dads, when the Lord asked this question of Satan, he was staking his name and reputation on Job. Could the Lord ask the same question of you and I? Could God say, "Have you considered my servant "_____?" You fill in the blank. Of Job, the Lord said, "There is no one on earth like him; he is blameless and upright, a man who fears God and shuns evil."

Within Satan's response to the God's question was a deep well of theological truths, although his conclusion was wrong. He said, "Does Job fear God for nothing?" In other words, was Job serving God only because of what he could get out of the relationship? As the meeting continued, Satan made another theological accusation: "Have you not put a hedge around him and his household and everything he has?" Now this is a theological truth; God does have a hedge of protection on and around those who are his in two forms: one in the person of the Holy Spirit who lives within us and secondly with the angels of the Lord who are encamped around us. (Psalm 34:7) Satan's second theologically true statement in his argument was "You have blessed the work of his hands, so that his flocks and herds are spread throughout the land." This is true; God does bless the work of his children and causes them to prosper in what they do. Lastly, Satan said, "If you stretch out your hand and strike everything he has, he will surely curse you to your face." What a powerful accusation and charge against Job. Satan was saying Job served God because of all the things God gave him and did for him. Herein is the underestimation of the power of God in the life of one of his children.

Dads, this divine meeting is complete with theological truths to be unfolded. Satan challenges God to remove the hedge from around Job; first mistake, to challenge God to do anything. God is sovereign, he is not responsible to do anything for anyone. What he does, he does because he chooses to do so, not because he has to or his character is in question if he does not. The Lord said to Satan, "Very well, then, everything he has is in your hands, but on the man himself do not lay a finger." In this response is a deep well of biblical truth. Dads, notice, if you will, that Satan had to have permission to attack Job. The enemy of our soul cannot do anything to one of

God's children without God's permission, and he can only go as far as God will allow him. His limit was "…but on the man himself do not lay a finger." In all that Job would go through, there was never a moment when God was not in control, and, dads, there is never a moment when you and I are going through trials that God is not in control. No matter how out of control things may appear, God is always in control.

The Four Messengers: Job 1:13 - 18

1. One day while Job's sons and daughters were feasting at the oldest son's house a messenger came to Job with news about his herds. "The oxen were plowing and the donkeys were grazing nearby, and the Sabeans attacked and carried them off. They put the servants to the sword, and I am the only one who has escaped to tell you."

2. While he was still speaking, another messenger came and said, "The fire of God fell from the sky and burned up the sheep and the servants, and I am the only one who has escaped to tell you!"

3. While he was still speaking another messenger came and said, "The Chaldeans formed three raiding parties and swept down on your camels and carried them off. They put the servants to the sword, and I am the only one who has escaped to tell you!"

4. While he was still speaking, yet another messenger came and said, "Your sons and daughters were feasting and drinking wine at the oldest brother's house, when suddenly a mighty wind swept in from the desert and struck the four corners of the house. It collapsed on them and they are dead, and I am the only one who has escaped to tell you!"

In spite of all that happened to Job, God was still in control. Job lost everything he owned, including his 10 children. I suspect that most of us would have been going out of our minds by this time, and Satan was certain that by now Job would have cursed God to his face. But not Job, he responded with his own fourfold response:

1.   Job got up and tore his robe, symbolizing his inner struggle and severe shock at what just happened to him for no apparent reason.
2.   Secondly, he shaved his head, which depicted the loss of his personal glory.
3.   Thirdly, he fell to the ground and worshiped God.
4.   He acknowledged that as he came into the world he would leave this world, he concluded that the Lord had given and the Lord had taken away; but even in the midst of all that happened, the name of the Lord was to be praised.

Dads, when you and I think we are at the bottom and life seems like it can't get any worse, unfortunately, sometimes it does, as was the case with Job. We have been programmed through television and radio to see life through 30-minute windows, and if troubles don't clear up in short time spans, we are ready to give up on God and others. Job teaches us that while troubles don't last always, they can be severe and continuous. But we have to hold on and not give up.

Meeting Number Two
Job 2:1-10

On another day the angels came to present themselves before the Lord, and Satan came with them to present himself as well. Once again, Satan answered God's question of his whereabouts, and he gave the same response as he did the first time God asked him; "From roaming through the earth and going back and forth in it."

NIV In the first Epistle of 1 Peter 5:8, the Scripture describes what Satan was doing in the earth; "Your enemy the devil prowls around like a roaring lion looking for someone to devour." NIV The Lord asked Satan a slightly different question during meeting number two; "Have you considered my servant Job? There is no one on earth like him; he is blameless and upright, a man who fears God and shuns evil. And still maintains his integrity, though you incited me against him, to ruin him without any reason." The Lord said, although he allowed Satan to test Job's integrity, without a reason to do so, Job was still standing upright in his integrity. The meeting continued with Satan responding to the Lord by accusing Job of being a callous man willing to give up the life of his animals, his servants and even his children to save his own life when he uses the phrase, "Skin for skin!" He said a man will give all that he has to save his own life. Satan again charged God that if he stretched out his hand and struck his flesh and bones, Job would surely curse God to his face. Once again, God granted permission, but his life was to be spared. Dads, there are times when God allows us to endure severe testing so that when we have been tested, we come through as refined gold ready to be adorned. Although Job was a great man and there was none like him in the earth, he still needed to be tested. Maybe not in the same way or to the same degree, but if you and I are to be what God would have us be we should expect to be tested.

Job's second round of testing began by Satan afflicting him with painful sores from the soles of his feet to the top of his head. He became so badly scarred that the one remaining person in his life who should have been standing with him, his wife, told him, "Are you still holding on to your integrity? Curse God and die!" Job told his wife, "You are talking like a foolish woman. Shall we accept good from God and not trouble?" In all this, Job did not sin in what he said. Dads, sometimes the people closest to us do not understand what God is doing with us when he is putting us through tests. Think back to when Abraham took his son Isaac up to Mount Moriah to present him to God as a living sacrifice. Do you think for a second that had Sarah known about the test God was putting Abraham through that she would have agreed with him sacrificing their son? Absolutely not! However, whether our wives understand or not is not our responsibility; our responsibility is to obey God and maintain our integrity with him.

Job's third test came from another unlikely source - his friends. After seven days of mourning, Job finally spoke but did not curse God, he, instead, cursed the day he was born. Job had a flaw in his theology; he, like his three friends, believed that the righteous get blessed and the wicked get punished. The fact that he had lost all that he possessed seemed to indicate that he had been punished as though he were one of the wicked when, in fact, he was certain that he was not. However, certain Job was, his three friends, Eliphaz, Bildad and Zophar, were not certain at all that Job and his children did not get what was coming to them. Dads, many times your closest friends do not understand when God is doing something behind the scene in your life.

As a result of all that he suffered, Job became very despondent with his station in life, but he never stopped believing in God, however flawed his theology. As Job contended with his three friends, he began to justify what he believed about God and suggested that God had not dealt justly with him. In Job 27:2-6, Job said, "As surely as God lives, who has denied me justice; the Almighty, who has made me taste bitterness of soul; as long as I have life within me, the breath of God in my nostrils; my lips will not speak wickedness, and my tongue will utter no deceit." Job said, "I will never admit you are in the right; till I die, I will not deny my integrity. I will maintain my righteousness and never let go of it; my conscience will not reproach me as long as I live." NIV Dads, sometimes we can become so engulfed in what we think to be true of God that we fail to recognize the sovereignty of God which cannot be contained within our limited understanding of him. It's no doubt that Job was a great man and that he was a righteous man, but he had a flawed theology that did not fully comprehend the vastness of sovereignty.

While Job never cursed God to his face as Satan said he would, Job did make some vital errors in the midst of his trials. Probably the most vital error Job made was to take stock of the man he once was and all of his accomplishments and his station in life. How many men do you know who put all that they are in their station in life?

Man of the Decade

In Job 29, Job began his lengthy monologue with God, speaking of the days when God watched over him; when God's lamp shone upon his head and how he walked by the light of God. He talked about when he was in his prime and had an intimate relationship with God and how God had blessed his house with children and how he loved to have them around. Job spoke of his standing in the community and how he was revered at the city gates and in the public square; how young men saw him and stepped aside and old men rose to their feet and the elders waited to speak and how he silenced voices of nobles and how everyone spoke well of him. Job rehearsed the good that he had done for the poor, the fatherless and the widows, those who were blind and lame; he spoke of how he was a father to the fatherless and a help to the stranger and he was the protector of those who were endangered. Job spoke of what he believed his glory on earth would have been and how men listened expectantly for his counsel. His words were the final words; he said that men waited for his words as men wait for showers of rain; his smile upon a person was a precious commodity. Job said he once dwelt as a king among his troops; he was like one who comforts mourners. In today's society Job would no doubt be the top candidate for man of the decade.

Dads, some of us are like Job, we do all the right things, but we lack understanding of the sovereignty of God; so God often sends an Elihu into our life to get us back on track. What is an Elihu, you ask? Elihu was a young man filled with the spirit of God and the wisdom to correct an old man. Elihu said to Job, "Far be it from God to do evil, from the Almighty to do wrong." NIV (Job 34:10b) Elihu gave four speeches to Job and his three friends to correct their thinking about God and he answered the question of God's justice. Elihu assured Job that the wicked will get his just due and that God never takes his eyes off the righteous. Elihu challenged Job to look at the wonders of God's power in the heavens and answer the question is God just. Elihu said that God loads the clouds with moisture; he scatters his lightning through them. At his direction, they swirl around over the face of the whole earth to do whatever he commands them. He brings the clouds to punish men, or to water his earth and show his love. He asked Job, "Do you know how God controls the clouds and makes his lightning flash? Do you know how the clouds hang poised, those wonders of him who is perfect in knowledge?" NIV (Job 37:15,16)

There are times, dads, when the Elihu in our life is not enough and God has to speak for himself as was the case with Job. When we go through trials sometimes the best thing for us to do is to keep silent, keep our thoughts to ourselves, because more often than not when we speak, we speak out of ignorance, and we say things that move us from being tested by God to being in trouble with God. The Lord decided that he had heard enough and answered Job out the storm. He said:

> Who is this that darkens my counsel with words without knowledge? Brace yourself like a man; I will question you, and you shall answer me.
> Where were you when I laid the earth's foundation? Tell me if you understand. Who marked off its dimensions? Surely you know! Who stretched a measuring line across it? On what were its footings set, or who laid its cornerstone – while the morning stars sang together and all the angels shouted for joy? Who shut up the sea behind doors when it burst

forth from the womb, when I made the clouds its garment and wrapped it in thick darkness, when I fixed limits for it and set its doors and bars in place, when I said, 'This far you may come and no farther; here is where your proud waves halt'? Have you ever given orders to the morning, or shown the dawn its place, that it might take the earth by the edges and shake the wicked out of it?

...Have you journeyed to the springs of the sea or walked in the recesses of the deep? Have the gates of death been shown to you? Have you seen the gates of the shadow of death? Have you comprehended the vast expanses of the earth? Tell me, if you know all this. What is the way to the abode of light? And where does darkness reside? Can you take them to their places? Do you know the paths to their dwellings? Surely you know, for you were already born! You have lived so many years!

Have you entered the storehouses of the snow or seen the storehouses of the hail, which I reserve for times of trouble, for days of war and battle? What is the way to the place where the lightning is dispersed, or the place where the east winds are scattered over the earth? Who cuts a channel for torrents of rain, and a path for the thunderstorm, to water a land where no man lives, a desert with no one in it, to satisfy a desolate wasteland and make it sprout with grass? NIV (Job 38:1-27)

It is apparent that we, like Job, are not capable of answering God's questions about things that He alone knows. One more time God would tell Job to "Brace himself like a man!" Dads, when you and I began to question God as to why he allows certain things to occur in our lives, we need to be prepared to do what he instructed Job to do and that is "Brace yourself like a man!"

Any man going through trials or testing, I encourage you to read the book of Job. Not only will you discover great things about the sovereignty of God, but you will discover great truths about his creative process as well. You will also discover that God is always in control regardless of how things may appear at the time of your trial or testing. After Job acknowledged that there was nothing that God could not do and that none of his purposes could be thwarted and that he had spoken about things of which he had no understanding, the Scripture records that the Lord blessed Job's latter days more than his former days. His brothers and sisters and all who knew him before came back and fellowshipped with him and ate at his table. His blessings were twofold:

- He lost 7,000 sheep; when God restored him, he gave him 14,000 sheep.
- He lost 3,000 camels; God gave him back 6,000 camels.
- He lost 500 yoke of oxen; God gave him back 1,000 yoke of oxen.
- He lost 500 donkeys; the Lord restored him with 1,000 female donkeys.
- Job lost his 10 children, seven sons and three daughters; God replaced his 10 children with 10 more children; seven more sons and three more daughters who were the most beautiful women in all the land. However, God did not stop there; he blessed Job with an inheritance for his children and his children's children. Job lived another 140 years and saw his sons and four generations of grandsons. And Job died an old man full of days.

In all that occurred in Job's life, there was never a time when God was not in full control. God was in control of Job's life's circumstances until the day he died. So dad, "Brace yourself like a man!" God is in control!

Lessons Learned from Job the Man of Integrity:

1. The trials that God allows in our lives have a higher purpose of which we are normally unaware.
2. God places His hedge of protection around those who are His.
3. God blesses the work of His children and causes them to prosper.
4. Never underestimate the power of God in the life of His children.
5. Satan's attacks on your life are subject to God's restrictive authority.
6. There is never a time when God is not aware and in control of my life's circumstances.
7. Trials will not last forever, although they may become severe and they may appear continuous.
8. God's testing process is for the purpose of refinement in the believer's life.
9. God never takes his eyes off His children.
10. God is always in control regardless of how things may appear at the time of your trial or during your test.

CHAPTER XV

Lessons Learned from Jesse —
The Father of the Anointed King of Israel

When I first identified Jesse as a dad in the Scriptures from whom we could glean parenting lessons, I thought to myself there really is not much here; the lesson was pretty clear and fairly obvious, "Don't look at the outward appearance." However, I quickly learned that not only was my view too limited, but I was thinking too small; after all Jesse was the father of a King. Jesse was the son of Obed and the grandson of Ruth the Moabite and Boaz the "Kinsman Redeemer." There are two books in the Bible that bear female names, the book of Esther and the book of Ruth, who was Jesse's grandmother. Jesse had a spiritual lineage that can be traced back to Adam and projected forward to Jesus Christ. By occupation, he was a farmer who lived in the town of Bethlehem in Judah and was from the tribe of Judah; he and his eight sons bred sheep. We are introduced to Jesse when Samuel the Priest came to Bethlehem to seek out and anoint a king to replace Israel's King Saul whom God had rejected from being king. (1 Samuel 15:23)

King Saul's partial obedience, which amounted to full disobedience, resulted in him being rejected by God, which led to the Lord turning his attention to selecting a new king to replace King Saul. Samuel was dispatched to Bethlehem to the house of Jesse to anoint the one that God would show him to be king over Israel. Why the Lord chose the house of Jesse was his sovereign choice, but it was there that the Lord's anointed replacement would be found. Upon Samuel's arrival in Bethlehem, he was greeted by the elders of the town, and they wanted to know if Samuel had come in peace or was he coming to pronounce judgment upon them for some reason. To demonstrate that he came in peace, Samuel invited the elders along with Jesse to consecrate themselves and offer a sacrifice with him before the Lord.

Dads, it is at this point that we learn our first lesson from Jesse about parenting through a biblical grid. The Scripture records that, "Then he consecrated Jesse and his sons and invited them to the sacrifice." NIV (1 Sam.16:5) Jesse was a consecrated man. In other words, Jesse was a man who was set apart for the service of the Lord. He was a humble man. As Jesse and his sons were set apart for God's use, you and I must also be willing to be set apart for service in God's kingdom. Jesse's humility was also evident by his profession; he was a farmer and a shepherd. This was the profession of common people; nobility did not shepherd sheep.

Dad, the second lesson we learn from Jesse is that real dads lead their families and their families follow their leadership. When Samuel arrived at Jesse's home and had Jesse bring his sons before him for evaluation and to go through the selection process, neither Jesse nor any of his sons wavered. Jesse's sons were not little boys, as one might think, they were grown men, but when their father had them come before Samuel the Priest, neither of them said a word against the idea of going before the priest; each son did as his dad asked. After seven of Jesse's sons had passed before Samuel and none were selected, Samuel asked Jesse "Are these all the sons you have?" Jesse replied, "There is still the youngest, but he is tending the sheep." Samuel instructed Jesse to call for David while they waited. When David arrived, he was "ruddy, with a fine appearance and handsome features." And the Lord told Samuel, "Rise and anoint him; he is the one." So Samuel anointed David in the presence of his brothers, and from that day forward the Spirit of the Lord came upon David; Jesse's leadership in the family led to the blessing of the family. Dads, by extension, we learn that our leadership in our families can and often times does lead to the blessing of our families.

The third lesson that we learn from Jesse is wisdom. Although God had rejected Saul as king, he had not yet removed Saul from the position. On a side note, this goes to show you that when the Lord declares something as done, you can count on it; even though it may not have happened yet, you can be sure that it will. The Scripture says Saul continued to function as the king for some time after the Spirit of the Lord had departed from him, and an evil spirit from the Lord tormented him. However, the one thing that would calm King Saul was the quiet playing of music, so he had his attendants seek out someone who was skillful at playing the harp. One of King Saul's attendants recalled seeing Jesse's son David play the harp, and when he informed the king, he was told to send for David. King Saul sent a messenger to Jesse requesting that he send his son David to play for him. The reigning king, who is soon to be replaced, requests the service of the one who has been anointed to replace him. When you know that your son is the anointed replacement of the rejected one, what do you do? Herein lies Jesse's wisdom. Jesse did the wisest thing he could have done; he acted as if Samuel had never visited his home and anointed his son to be king. He sent his son David as the king requested, and he sent him bearing gifts.

The hidden wisdom in what Jesse did reveals that although God may give you a glimpse of what He is going to do, that does not mean that you get ahead of Him. Some years ago I received an unexpected startling email from a senior executive; the message rocked me to my core. I needed to reply to the email but before I could reply I had to pray, because my response could have been career limiting, if not ending. I left my office and went to a park that I often retreat to for prayer and I prayed about my response. I returned to my office and sent my response, which was brief and to the point. Still reeling from the jolt, later that evening while at home, I entered a very serious time of prayer about the situation. Now, as I was praying, as clear as day, I heard in my heart the Lord tell me that the person who sent me the jolting email was gone. It was so clear that it startled me. I immediately prayed, telling the Lord that I didn't want to see anyone to be in harm's way, I just wanted my name to be vindicated. Again, the Lord said the person was gone. I was so happy when I returned to work the following Monday to discover that the person was at work and was not gone. However, in less than a year that person's last day with the company was announced. How we respond once God has spoken is as important as our response before he speaks.

The final lesson that Jesse teaches us is that it is not about us, but rather it is about what is produced from us. Jesse's fatherhood was about what his son David would become. If it were not for David becoming the king of Israel, Scripture has no need to mention Jesse's name. Jesse is important not for who he was, but for who he produced. The writer of the Book of Acts records that,

> After removing Saul, he made David their king. He testified concerning him: I have found David, son of Jesse, a man after my own heart; he will do everything I want him to do. From this man's descendants God has brought to Israel the Savior Jesus, as he promised. NIV (Acts 13:22-23)

Jesse produced a son who was said to have a heart that reflected the heart of God. According to Isaiah 11:1-5, a shoot or rod, that humble little growth, and a branch will spring from the stem or root of Jesse and it will bear fruit. What we want as dads is to see our kids bear fruit. You see what came from Jesse was a son named David, in whom God saw the reflection of his own heart. I believe Jesse had significant influence on how David developed into a man and Jesse's influence on David's life allowed God to trust David with the kingdom. Regarding David, the Scripture says:

> The Spirit of the Lord will rest on him – the Spirit of wisdom and the Spirit of understanding, the Spirit of counsel and of power, the Spirit of knowledge and of the fear of the Lord– and he will delight in the fear

of the Lord. He will not judge by what he sees with his eyes, or decide by what he hears with his ears; but with righteousness he will judge the needy, with justice he will give decisions for the poor of the earth. He will strike the earth with the rod of his mouth; with the breath of his lips he will slay the wicked. Righteousness will be his belt and faithfulness the sash around his waist. NIV (Isaiah 11:2-5)

Dads, the primary lesson I learned from Jesse's life as a parent is that it's not about me; it's about what I produce. How well do my children reflect me? Do your sons and daughters reflect you and, if so, what is in that reflection? Jesse came from good stock; his parents, grandparents and great-grandparents were people of faith, and he would pass that faith on to his sons and grandsons for many generations to follow. Not only would he pass on his faith in Jehovah, but the royal lineage would pass from his son David to Solomon and to Rehoboam and later on to Uzziah and King Hezekiah and the young king, Josiah, who became king at the age of eight. Finally, after 28 generations, the royal lineage would produce Jesus the Messiah who will forever be seated on the throne of David. While Jesse may not have started out looking like much more than a farmer and sheep herder, once he was consecrated to the Lord he became the father of kings and kingdoms. Dads, as Jesse's life illustrates, where you start does not dictate where you will finish.

Lessons Learned from Jesse:

1. **Dads, the blessings of the Lord come after the consecration of our hearts and our families.**
2. **Real dads are the spiritual leaders of their family.**
3. **Do not get ahead of God. Although God may have declared something, wait on His fulfillment.**

4. It's not about us, it's about the fruit that we bear and how that fruit reflects our influence.
5. Your beginning does not necessarily determine your ending; your choices will influence how your story will end.

CHAPTER XVI

Lessons Learned from David — King of Israel and Judah

What is the measure of a man? The Scriptures say something about David, who was arguably Israel's greatest king, that has always given me pause. What it says about King David begs the question of what is the measure of a man? From God's perspective, what is it that defines who we are? Are we to be defined by an incident or a moment in our life or are we defined by the amalgamation of incidents in their totality or is it something else by which we are defined? King David's life causes one to ask a series of questions about God, that when answered provide us with life lessons:

- Does God overlook certain sins?
- Why do the innocent suffer?
- How can those who are flawed be righteous?
- Why are the strong also the weak?
- Who has the ear of the King?
- Can a man separate his occupation from his family obligation?
- What are a man's responsibilities to his family regardless of his position?
- How did David's blended family affect his kingdom and legacy?
- How did his sin affect his family?
- How did righteousness affect his family and his kingdom?
- How was David a man after God's own heart?

It is through ones search for answers to these questions and many others that one also learns lessons for parenting from a faith-based approach.

King David was sought out by God and anointed king over Israel after his predecessor, King Saul, failed to keep the commands of God when he violated the office of the priesthood by offering burnt offerings and fellowship offerings before the Lord before engaging in battle with his nemeses the Philistines. Saul failed to wait on Samuel the Priest to come and present the offerings, and he overstepped his authority as king and became both king and priest, for which he had no authority. Because of Saul's foolish actions, God rejected him as king and sought out and found David, the shepherd of his father's sheep, and anointed him king over Israel. The Lord asked Samuel, "How long will you mourn for Saul, since I have rejected him as king over Israel? Fill your horn with oil and be on your way; I am sending you to Jesse of Bethlehem. I have chosen one of his sons to be king." NIV (1 Samuel 16:1)

Dads, one of the first things we learn from King David is that how we appear is not what impresses God. When the Lord sent Samuel to Bethlehem to search out Saul's replacement, one of the first things he told Samuel was not to look on the appearance of a man. Samuel was told that, "The Lord does not look at the things man looks at. Man looks at the outward appearance, but the Lord looks at the heart." NIV (1 Samuel 16:7) It amazes me that we get dressed up in our thousand dollar suits and live in our big houses and drive our fancy cars to impress others, but God is not impressed. Dads, the Lord wants men and women who will do what he asks of them. In David, the Lord found such a man.

Although David did what God asked him to do, some of his actions begs the question what is the measure of a man? David lived a life that can be characterized by the great and mighty things that he did and the tremendous victories that he won for his nation, beginning with his victorious battle over the Philistine giant named Goliath. When David became king of Israel, he was for many years a warrior king; his kingdom reign was fraught with battles against many enemies. In fact, when he sought to build the temple for the Lord, the Lord said that he could not because he had shed blood, but he would allow his son, Solomon, to build his temple.

However mighty David was as king of Israel, he was also flawed, which begs the question: Does God overlook certain sins or flaws in our character? King David had a major flaw that I believe profoundly impacted not only his life but his family's life and the health of his nation. He practiced polygamy. King David had eight wives that we know by name and the Scripture says that he had many others, including his harem of concubines. These eight wives – Ahinoam, Abigail, Maacah, Haggith, Abital, Eglah, Michal and Bathsheba – gave King David 19 sons and several daughters. While polygamy was a common practice among the ancient patriarchs, it was not God's plan and purpose for marriage nor were those who practiced polygamy absolved from its consequences. Polygamy always brought with it infighting, jealousies, hatred and severe family dysfunctionality.

How did God, or did God, overlook David's character flaw and his practice of what God clearly seemed to prohibit in the confines of marriage and he himself remain righteous? How did God use this flawed man? Can God overlook sin and he himself remain righteous? I believe we find the answers to these age-old questions in the words of Scripture found in the writings of the prophet Isaiah. "For my thoughts are not your thoughts, neither are your ways my ways," declares the Lord. "As the heavens are higher than the earth, so are my ways higher than your ways and my thoughts than your thoughts." NIV (Isaiah 55:8-9) I don't believe that God overlooked King David's character flaws that led to his sin, but rather God used his character flaws to reveal his sin. King David's flaw was his eye for beauty; his sin was to marry multiple women. However, the Scripture tells us that his heart was always toward God.

I guess one of the most fascinating stories that demonstrates this flaw is the story of David and Bathsheba. Many of us learned this story in our childhood days of Sunday School and Vacation Bible

Study. It is an intriguing story of beauty, deceit, destruction, courage and forgiveness. The story of David and Bathsheba took place not long after King David had accomplished a tremendous victory over the Ammonites. The Scripture says that David and his men fought against them and killed seven hundred of their charioteers and forty thousand of their foot soldiers along with their commander. Those who were once their enemies became subject to them. The Ammonites were defeated and their allies no longer came to their aid after this horrendous defeat.

However, there is a shift of events that occurs after this tremendous victory. The Scripture says, "In the spring, at the time when kings go off to war, David sent Joab out with the king's men and the whole Israelite army. They destroyed the Ammonites and besieged Rabbah. But David remained in Jerusalem." NIV (2 Samuel 11:1) It was while King David remained in Jerusalem that he encountered Bathsheba. King David should have been where kings were during the spring – on the battlefield with his army. However, he chose to send his commander and remain in Jerusalem in his palace. Dads, let me pause here a say that we should always be where we belong, when we belong there. When I worked nights for many years, I would often tell my colleagues that the best thing we could do when we got off work was to go home, and to go straight home, because too many things can happen when we are not where we are supposed to be.

It was during this time when King David wasn't where he should have been that he saw the most beautiful woman he had ever laid eyes on, Bathsheba. From his rooftop, King David saw her at home bathing, and he had someone inquire about her to find out who she was. One of the king's servants said, "Isn't this Bathsheba, the daughter of Eliam and the wife of Uriah the Hittite?" NIV (11:3) King David then sent for her and he brought her into the palace and he slept with her and she became pregnant. Tremendous victory was followed by a horrendous failure. Let me share four things that King David knew: 1.) He knew that he was where he should not have been at that time. He should have been on the battlefield where kings are during the spring. 2.) He knew, after inquiring about her, that Bathsheba was the daughter of Eliam, who was the son of Ahithophel, who had been one of his closes counselors and advisors. So she was the granddaughter of his counselor and advisor. 3.) He knew that she was married to Uriah the Hittite. 4.) He knew that Uriah was one of his elite soldiers listed among his thirty bodyguards and elite fighting men. King David did not go into his act of adultery with his eyes closed; he knew exactly what he was doing and with whom he was doing it. Dads, King David shows that we never fall into sin, but that we go in with our eyes wide open and fully aware. What we don't do is go into sin with a clear understanding of its cost.

King David, like many a man and woman have attempted, tried to cover up his sin. He was the king, he was smart, and he had authority, so he would simply have Bathsheba's husband come in from the battlefield and surely he would take the opportunity to spend some personal time with his wife and who will be the wiser. Bathsheba would give birth and Uriah would be a proud poppa and no one would ever know the difference. It sounded like the king had a workable plan that would disguise his sin. God's plan to reveal the king's character flaw was to make Uriah a more honorable man than the king. Uriah was brought in from the battlefield to meet with the king and after the king inquired about the battle and how the men were doing, he told Uriah to go home and "wash your feet." NIV (11:8) King David was suggesting that Uriah go home and relax with his wife, who, after all, was beautiful and he had not seen for a while, and be intimate with her.

The Scripture says that Uriah left the king's presence, but he went and slept at the entrance to the palace with all of his master's servants and did not go to his house. I suspect his master's servants could give testimony to his actions if called upon to do so. The king's plan to deceive Uriah and mask his sin was not working. The next day King David summoned Uriah back to the palace to question him about his actions the night before. David wanted to know why Uriah had not gone to be with his wife. The response that Uriah gave was more honorable than the king's actions. Uriah told King David, "The ark and Israel and Judah are staying in tents, and my master Joab and my Lord's men are camped in the open fields. How could I go to my house to eat and drink and lie with my wife? As surely as you live, I will not do such a thing!" NIV (11:11) Uriah at this point proved to be a man of honor while the man after God's own heart was acting dishonorably.

When David saw that his first plan to deceive failed, he decided to try another approach and he insisted that Uriah stay one more night. However, this time he would throw in a little celebration and have Uriah eat at his table and drink with him even to the point of getting him drunk. The king thought surely if he got Uriah intoxicated, he would forget his vow and go home and sleep with his wife; after all she was very beautiful and she was his wife. But once again Uriah, even in his drunken state, was cognizant enough to remember his vow, and he slept on a mat among his master's servants; he did not go home.

In the morning when King David realized that his second attempt to deceive Uriah did not work, he set in motion a plan to destroy him. The king wrote a letter to Joab, the commander of his army, telling him to put Uriah on the front line where the fighting was the fiercest, and, to be certain that Uriah would be killed, Joab was instructed to then withdraw from him so he would be struck down and die. For the king thought surely if Uriah was dead, then his sin would be covered. The king sent the letter to Joab by Uriah. This was the man after God's own heart. King David's plan seemed to work, Uriah was killed and David's sin was covered. He later sent messengers to Bathsheba and informed her that her husband was killed in battle. After Bathsheba's period of mourning was over, David had her brought to the palace and he married her and they had a son. But the things that David did displeased the Lord.

Dads, no matter how much we think we have done to cover up our sin, God never lets sin go unpunished or unchecked. The price for our sins has been paid on the cross; that is what Jesus died for, however, before his payment can be applied to our personal account with God, he sometimes has to use someone to get our attention. In David's case he used Nathan the prophet. Dads, let me offer this advice: unless you are specifically appointed by God to be used in this way, don't go around trying to check people about their sin. Take the beam out of your own eye first before you try to pluck the speck out of your brother's eyes. God sent Nathan to get King David's attention. Also, in the case of those in authority and power, it would do you well to be of equal authority and power before you go trying to correct others. Nathan was David's equal in the sense that it was understood and accepted that they were both men appointed and anointed by God for their office. In David's day there were basically four offices: king, priest, prophet and judge, each of which had standing throughout Israel and Judah.

Nathan was courageous. I named our son Nathan after the prophet in hopes that he would in time gain not only the wisdom of the prophet Nathan but also his courage. After the king and his new bride were settled in the palace, Nathan paid him a visit to tell him a story about a rich man and a poor man. In short, the story was that these two men lived in the same town, one had all kinds of riches, he had a large number of sheep and a large number of cattle, but the poor man had nothing to speak of except one little ewe lamb that he had bought. He raised this ewe lamb and it was precious to him; he cared for it, in fact, it slept in his arms, it was like a daughter to him. On one occasion, a traveler was passing by and the rich man, who had plenty of sheep and cattle, prepared a meal for the traveler, but instead of using one of his many animals to feed the traveler he took the lamb that belonged to the poor man and prepared it for the traveler. King David burned with anger when he heard that story and said to Nathan:

> "As surely as the Lord lives, the man who did this
> deserves to die! He must pay for that lamb four
> times over, because he did such a thing and had
> no pity." Then Nathan said to David, "You are the

man! This is what the Lord, the God of Israel, says:
'I anointed you king over Israel, and I delivered you
from the hand of Saul. I gave your master's house to
you, and your master's wives into your arms.
I gave you the house of Israel and Judah. And if all
this had been too little, I would have given you even
more. Why did you despise the word of the Lord by
doing what is evil in his eyes? You struck down Uriah
the Hittite with the sword and took his wife to be your
own. You killed him with the sword of the Ammonites.
Now, therefore, the sword will never depart from your
house, because you despised me and took the wife of
Uriah the Hittite to be your own.' "This is what the
Lord says: 'Out of your own household I am going to
bring calamity upon you. Before your very eyes I will
take your wives in broad daylight." You did it in secret,
but I will do this thing in broad daylight before all
Israel." NIV (2 Samuel 12:5-12)

Then David told Nathan, "I have sinned against the Lord."
Nathan assured David that his sin had been forgiven because of
his repentant heart, but because of his sin, he made the Lord's
enemies to show contempt. As a result, the son who was born to he
and Bathsheba died. The innocent child died because of the sinful
actions of its father. Why do the innocent suffer? In this case, the
innocent suffered so that the guilty pay a price for their actions.

The lesson of David and Bathsheba teaches us that sin can
never be covered up no matter how hard we try. It also teaches us
that when we are out of place we put ourselves in danger of seeing
and doing that from which we would otherwise be insulated. David
and Bathsheba's encounter also teaches us that sin is progressive in
nature. Being out of place was the first thing David did wrong; not
watching what he allowed himself to see was the next thing he did
wrong; then he invited sin into his house; once the act was complete,

he then attempted to cover it up; when that failed, he destroyed that which would expose his sin; and then he became comfortable in his sin. Lastly, David and Bathsheba's encounter teaches us that forgiveness is available and possible to the repentant heart, but sin never leaves us without leaving its consequences behind.

Although the incident with Bathsheba and Uriah marked King David's life and reign as king of Israel and Judah, it did not define him. God had already defined him. In Psalms 51 and 32, we are given a glimpse into the heart of David, as they are the extended verbiage of his confession. In these Psalms, David pleaded for God's mercy and unfailing love to be restored to him. He called upon God to wash him with hyssop, which was a cleaning agent; he confessed that his transgressions and his sin were always before him. In other words, David was saying to God not only did I sin, but I knew the line was there and I stepped over the line anyway. When we transgress, we see the line, we know where the line is, and we choose to step over the line anyway. David said he saw the line and he stepped over it anyway and when he did, he went further and committed acts of sin. He even said that he had been sinful from his birth. King David's sin caused him to lose the joy and gladness that he once enjoyed; he prayed that God would restore that joy. In his prayer, King David asked God to create in him a pure heart and he asked that his spirit be renewed. He pleaded with God not to cast him off from his presence or take from him his Holy Spirit. David asked him to restore the joy of his salvation; his contention was that if God restored him then he would be able to teach others not to do what he had done. In Psalm 32, King David said that when he kept silent about his sin, his bones wasted away and he literally hurt all the time because God's hand was heavy upon him. His strength was sapped as in the heat of summer. However, he said when he confessed his sin, God forgave him of the guilt of his sin.

After King David was forgiven and his relationship with God restored, he and Bathsheba continued on with their family life and they had another son, Solomon, who would become heir to the throne. However, because David practiced polygamy, his family life was fraught with myriads of dysfunctionality. Because so much emphasis is placed on the events that occurred between David and Bathsheba, it is easy to forget that King David had at least seven other wives, six of whom gave him children. The daughter of King Saul, Michal, who was given to David in marriage, was his only wife who did not have any children. Had she given King David children, his kingdom would have been in constant jeopardy of being overthrown. Furthermore, King David had an unknown amount of concubines. His children who we know of included: Amnon, Kileab, Absalom, Adonijah, Shephatatiah, Ithream, Shammua, Shobab, Nathan, Solomon, Ibhar, Elishua, Nepheg, Japhia, Elishama, Eliada, Eliphelet, Tamar and the child that he and Bathsheba had who the Lord struck with an illness and it died. Today, we would say that King David had a blended family. While there is nothing inherently wrong with blended families, they do pose unique challenges for parents; King David's family was no different.

Let's examine the dysfunctionality of King David's blended family. It began with his first born son, Amnon, who fell in love with his half-sister, Tamar, who was the sister of his brother Absalom by King David's wife Maacah the Canaanite. Not only did King David marry multiple women, but they had many different religious beliefs and practices. Today, in our age of tolerance, we say that one's religious beliefs and practices should not matter as long as we are "in love." Let me just say that religious beliefs and practices have always mattered, and they matter today. Amnon fell in love with his half-sister. He and King David's brother, Jonadab, devised a scheme in which Amnon would pretend to be ill and would arrange to have Tamar come and care for him. While she was caring for him, he took her by force and raped her, although she begged him not to take her by force. Tamar begged her brother to ask their father the king to allow them to marry so that they could live without shame, but he refused and took her by force. This act disgraced Tamar and made Amnon a criminal. The Scripture says that after Amnon raped his half-sister, he began to hate her with an intense hatred. In fact, it says that he hated her more than he loved her.

When Tamar could no longer wear the ornamented robe of the virgin daughters of the king, it became evident to her family that someone had been with her. When her brother Absalom realized what their brother Amnon had done, he burned with quiet vengeance. When King David heard all that Amnon had done, he was furious, however, he never took action against his son. However, Absalom spent two years carefully planning his revenge on his half-brother Amnon for what he had done to their sister Tamar. The time came when Absalom invited the sheepshearers from the surrounding area to a feast, and he called upon the king to join him along with his sons. While the king thought it unwise to join Absalom along with all of his sons, he permitted his sons to join Absalom and his men. Absalom had devised a diabolical plan to get his brothers drunk with wine, and when Amnon was in high spirits, he ordered his men to strike him dead. Absalom had to encourage his men to be strong and to be brave because there would be severe repercussions for killing one of the king's sons. The murder of Amnon by his brother's men frightened all the other brothers and they quickly fled from Absalom. Absalom had taken it upon himself to enact upon his brother what the law required for the crime of rape. Absalom did what his father, King David, was unwilling to do. Now Absalom was a fugitive.

Absalom spent three years as a fugitive from his father before returning to Jerusalem. However, after he returned, another two years passed before the king allowed him to see his face. While King David had been consoled concerning the death of his first born son Amnon, he was not prepared to see his murderer even though that murderer was his third son Absalom. After two years the king summoned Absalom and he made peace with him and he kissed him. However, over time Absalom had built his own forces and his own followers, and through his own deceptive practices he stole the hearts of the people and attempted to take over his father's kingdom. Absalom's revolt caused King David and his men to flee Jerusalem.

David took all that he had except for 10 of his concubines, whom he left behind to care for the palace.

An interesting thing happened while King David was on the run from his son who had taken over the throne and was ruling in Jerusalem as though he was the anointed king. As the self-appointed king of Israel, Absalom sought the advice of his father's trusted advisor Ahithophel, who, as you will recall, was also the grandfather of Bathsheba, whom King David had taken from her husband Uriah. You will also recall that in God's judgment of King David, the Lord said through the prophet Nathan that what King David did to Uriah in secret he would do to him in public. In other words, King David took Bathsheba in private, but God was going to allow King David's wives to be taken before all Israel in broad daylight. Well, Absalom asked Ahithophel for his best advice on how to continue to win over the allegiance of the people. Ahithophel told Absalom to "Lie with your father's concubines, whom he left to take care of the palace. Then all Israel will hear that you have made yourself a stench in your father's nostrils, and the hands of everyone with you will be strengthened." So they pitched a tent for Absalom on the rooftop, and he lay with his father's concubines in the sight of all Israel. The Scripture says, "Now in those days the advice Ahithophel gave was like that of one who inquires of God. That was how both David and Absalom regarded all of Ahithophel's advice. NIV (16:21-23) Although it was awful what Absalom did, it was exactly what God said would happen; what God did not reveal to King David or Nathan the prophet was that it would be the king's own son who would do such an evil dysfunctional thing.

Eventually King David and his army would have to face Absalom and his army. When they did, King David's men prevailed and defeated Absalom's army. Escaping, Absalom fled on his mule, but the mule ran under an oak tree and Absalom got stuck hanging from its branches. When Joab, the captain of King David's army, heard this, he and his men struck Absalom with javelins and killed him. However, when King David heard the news, he wept for his son and said, "O my son Absalom! My son, my son Absalom! If only I had died instead of you-O Absalom, my son, my son." NIV (18:33) Although Absalom had led a revolt and killed his father's first born son, he was still King David's son and his father loved him and he grieved his loss.

As King David grew old, his fourth son, Adonijah who was the son of Haggith, who was King David's fourth wife, put himself forward and said "I will be king." NIV (1 Kings 1:5) However, this time, before Adonijah could gain any traction with the people, Nathan the prophet and King David's wife Bathsheba executed their plan to have her son Solomon anointed as King David's successor to the throne. As time drew near for King David to die, he gave a charge to his son Solomon:

1. Be strong, show yourself a man and observe what the Lord your God requires.
2. Walk in his ways, and keep his decrees and commands, his laws and requirements, as written in the law of Moses, so that you may prosper in all you do and wherever you go, and that the Lord may keep his promise to me: "If your descendants watch how they live, and if they walk faithfully before me with all their heart and soul, you will never fail to have a man on the throne of Israel."
3. Deal with Joab according to your wisdom, but do not let his gray head go down to the grave in peace.
4. Show kindness to those who showed kindness to me.
5. Remember those who were my enemies and deal with them appropriately. NIV (1 Kings 2:2-9)

Although King David died and left the kingdom in the capable hands of Solomon, there was still the unfinished business of Adonijah, who made a second attempt to infiltrate the inner circle by requesting the hand in marriage of Abishag the Shunammite, who belonged to King David's harem. If Adonijah married one from the king's harem, he would be one step closer to taking the throne from his younger brother Solomon. Solomon quickly saw through Adonijah's plans and gave orders to have him killed.

King David's sin had dramatic effects on his family and their dysfunctionality just as our sin has dramatic effects on our families. Dads, you and I have to always remember that our decisions will impact our families in the present as well as the future. In all that happened in King David's life that seemed to be so horrible, and it was, God still said he was a man after his own heart.

How was David a man after God's own heart?

1. David would not lift his hands against the Lord's anointed king, even though God had rejected him. (1 Samuel 24:6)
2. King David reverenced the things of God; he brought the Ark of God to Jerusalem. (2 Samuel 6)
3. King David worshiped God openly through dance and songs of praise. (2 Samuel 6:16)
4. David sought to build a house for God that he might have a dwelling place before the people. (2 Samuel 7:1-17)
5. King David was humble before the Sovereign Lord. (2 Samuel 7:18-29)
6. The Scripture says that David reigned over all Israel, doing what was just and right for all the people. (2 Samuel 8:15)
7. David showed kindness to Jonathan's crippled son, Mephibosheth, because of the strong relationship he and Jonathan enjoyed. (2 Samuel 9:1-13)
8. David confessed his sin. (2 Samuel 12:13)
9. King David sought forgiveness for his sin. (Psalm 51)
10. King David acknowledged the effects of his sin and he praised the Lord for his forgiveness. (Psalm 32)

Although I could cite many more examples of how David was

a man after God's own heart, these 10 adequately demonstrate that in spite of his faults his heart was directed toward God.

Dads, we have to realize that although we all have flaws in our character, those flaws don't have to keep us from being used by God. What the Lord requires of us is not that we be perfect, but that we act justly and love mercy and to walk humbly with our God. Do these things and you will become a man after God's own heart; your children and your children's children will be blessed because you decided to walk with God.

Lessons Learned from David – King of Israel and Judah

1. Dads, how we appear to others is not what impresses God.
2. As dads, we need to always be where we belong, when we belong there.
3. Dads, King David shows that we never fall into sin; we go in with our eyes wide open and fully aware. What we don't do is go into sin with a clear understanding of its cost.
4. No matter how much we think we have done to cover up our sin, God never lets sin go unpunished or unchecked.
5. Dads, always remember to examine first yourself before trying to correct others about their sin.
6. Dads, you and I have to always remember that our decisions will impact our families in the present as well as the future.
7. Dads, we have to realize that even though we are flawed characters, our flaws don't have to keep us from being used by God.
8. Dads, if you want God to view you as a man after his own heart you must - Act Justly, Love Mercy and Walk Humbly with our God.

CHAPTER XVII

Lessons Learned from Joseph —
The Father who Raised Jesus

As I began to think about Joseph, the husband of Mary, the mother of our Lord Jesus Christ, I struggled with what to call him. While he was the husband of Mary, he was not the biological father of our Lord Jesus Christ. He was not his step father because in order to have a stepfather there had to be a biological father and there was not.

> In the sixth month, God sent the angel Gabriel to Nazareth, a town in Galilee, to a virgin pledged to be married to a man named Joseph, a descendant of David. The virgin's name was Mary. The angel went to her and said, "Greetings, you who are highly favored! The Lord is with you." Mary was greatly troubled at his words and wondered what kind of greeting this might be. But the angel said to her, "Do not be afraid, Mary, you have found favor with God. You will be with child and give birth to a son, and you are to give him the name Jesus. He will be great and will be called the Son of the Most High. The Lord God will give him the throne of his father David, and he will reign over the house of Jacob forever; his kingdom will never end." "How will this be," Mary asked the angel, "since I am a virgin?" The angel answered,

"The Holy Spirit will come upon you, and the power of the Most High will overshadow you. So the holy one to be born will be called the Son of God. NIV (Luke 1:26-35)

Jesus was conceived by the Holy Spirit. (Matthew 1:18) Some would call Joseph the foster dad of our Lord, however, the Scripture says he and Mary were the parents of our Lord even though Joseph was not his biological father. When Jesus was a boy just 12 years old, the Scripture says his parents took him to Jerusalem for the feast of the Passover. So, for purposes of this lesson I will simply refer to Joseph as the father who raised Jesus the Christ.

Jesus lived and grew up in a blended family. In our day and time blended families are a common reality for millions of families. Blended families exist as a result of a myriad of circumstances: the death of a spouse and remarriage, children born out of wedlock, divorce and remarriage, and adoption of children. Somehow none of these scenarios seem to measure up to the situation in which Joseph found himself. Joseph was engaged to be married to Mary when she was found to be with child by the Holy Spirit. However, Joseph, being a righteous man and not wanting to disgrace Mary, desired to put her away secretly. In the ancient tradition of Jewish marriages the period of engagement was actually a formal prenuptial contract that was entered into before several witnesses. This contract gave the man legal rights and responsibilities for his bride-to-be, which could only be broken by a formal process of divorce. Joseph found himself in a predicament; if he divorced Mary she could be subject to penalty for adultery because she would have been accused of breaking her marriage vow during the engagement period. If Joseph took her in and married her, they would have violated the normal one-year engagement period. Also, he would have to raise this child that he did not father.

The first lesson we learn from the life of Joseph is that before men become dads they need to become righteous men. Joseph was a righteous man. The Scripture says, "before they came together..." that is before they had sexual relations with one another she was found to be with child. NIV (Matthew 1:18) It amazes me today the arguments that are put forth for why couples should engage in premarital sexual relations. I am reminded of a situation that happened in my senior year of high school. If you will recall, I said earlier that I needed so many

Righteous Character

credit hours when I got to my senior year in high school that I took a lot of classes every day in both day and night school. Well, one of the classes I took was a class on fashion design that was predominantly a class of females. Within that class there was a young lady who let it slip out that she was still a virgin and had never been sexually involved, and I can vividly recall the other girls in the class teasing this girl to no end. I am certain that, as a young man, I did not feel then the way I feel now as a dad who has raised two daughters. As a dad, I say thank God it's not a crime for young ladies to remain virgins until they are married.

Another lesson that we learn from Joseph is that because he was a righteous man he considered a righteous solution to his dilemma. Joseph's righteous solution would be to quietly divorce Mary in the presence of two witnesses. This would allow him to both remain righteous and be charitable at the same time by not exposing Mary to the public at large. There is always a righteous solution to every situation. Observe God's righteous solution to Joseph's situation. Joseph, like any man would, had serious questions that needed to be answered: How can this be happening to me? What am I going to do? What about Mary and her family? Adultery in Joseph's day came with serious consequences. What if he raised the child secretly as his own biological son, who would know the difference? God's righteous solution was to send Joseph answers to the questions he no doubt had. "An angel of the Lord appeared to him in a dream, saying, 'Joseph, son of David, do not be afraid to take Mary as your wife; for that which has been conceived in her is of the Holy Spirit. And she will bear a Son; and you shall call His name Jesus, for it is He who will save His people from their sins." NIV (Matthew 1:20-21)

Let me make a couple of observations about God's righteous solution:

1. After Joseph had considered his own righteous alternative, God shared with him a better and more righteous solution. He sent an angel of the Lord to Joseph in a dream to let him know that there was no need for him to be afraid to take Mary home as his wife because what was happening with her was of God. I suspect that the angel of the Lord was the same angel who had come to both Mary and her cousin Elizabeth with the same information about the miraculous birth of John the Baptist who was the forerunner and cousin of the Lord Jesus.

2. The angel of the Lord legitimized the parenthood of Joseph. The angel referred to Joseph using his genealogical connection to Jesus when he called him "Joseph son of David." Not only was Joseph the father who would raise Jesus, but he was His legal genealogical father although he was not his biological father.

3. Joseph was a father who was willing to listen and obey the word of God. The Scripture says that Joseph arose from his sleep, and did as the angel of the Lord commanded him, and took her as his wife and he kept her a virgin until she gave birth to a Son; and he called His name Jesus. (Matthew 1:24-25)

The next lesson we learn from the life of Joseph is that his obedience to God led to the protection and preservation of his family. After the birth of Jesus, history and Scripture record that King Herod the Great sent Magi, "Wise Men," to inquire of the birth of Jesus Christ. In fact, Scripture says that he gathered the chief priests and scribes and inquired of them where the Christ was to be born. The Magi called Him "He who has been born King of the Jews." NASB (Matthew 2:1-4) Scripture also records that King Herod sought to kill Jesus after His birth and an angel of the Lord appeared to Joseph in a second dream, saying, "Arise and take the child and His

Righteous Response

mother, and flee to Egypt, and remain there until I tell you; for Herod is going to search for the child to destroy Him." And he arose and took the child and His mother by night, and departed for Egypt; and was there until the death of Herod, and so that which was spoken by the Lord through the prophet might be fulfilled, saying, "Out of Egypt did I call My Son." NASB (Matthew 2:13-15) Joseph's obedience to the word of God protected and preserved his family from

Righteous Outcomes

impending dangers. As a dad, I always told my kids that there is a real devil in the world and his purpose is threefold: to kill, steal and destroy. But, as a dad, it's my responsibility to be obedient to God if I want to protect and preserve my family from potential dangers and the schemes of the enemy of their soul.

The fourth life lesson we learn from Joseph is that obedience to God's word allows us to step into the determined will of God for our lives. After King Herod died, the Scripture says, "But when Herod was dead, behold an angel of the Lord appeared in a dream to Joseph in Egypt,

Righteous Solutions

saying, 'Arise and take the Child and His mother, and go into the land of Israel; for those who were trying to take the child's life are dead." NASB (Matthew 2:19-20) Further warnings in the dream instructed Joseph to take his family to the region of Galilee, and he went there and made their residence in a city called Nazareth, that what was spoken through the prophets might be fulfilled, "He shall be called a Nazarene."

Righteous Steps Ordered by God

NASB (Matthew 2:23) Dads who obey the word of God in all things will lead their families into the perfect will of God.

The Apostle Paul put it this way in Romans 12:1-2:

> Therefore, I urge you, brothers, in view of God's mercy, to offer your bodies as living sacrifices, holy and pleasing to God, this is your spiritual act of worship. Do not conform any longer to the pattern of this world, but be transformed by the renewing of your mind. Then you will be able to test and approve what God's will is, his good, pleasing and perfect will. NIV

The final life lesson we glean is from Joseph's family's journey to Jerusalem for the Feast of the Passover when Jesus was twelve years of age. The Scripture records that Joseph's family went up to Jerusalem, according to their custom of the Feast; and, when they were returning home, Jesus' parents, Joseph and Mary, discovered to their surprise that Jesus was no longer in the caravan after a couple days' journey. Upon their return to Jerusalem and spending several days searching the city for him, they found him sitting in the temple in the midst of the teachers, both listening to them and questioning them. Although Mary and Joseph had been anxiously looking for Him, Joseph handled the situation in such a way that Jesus did not lose or lack respect for Joseph's authority as His earthly parent. After three days of searching for Jesus, when they found him teaching in the temple, they were amazed and Mary said to him, "Son, why have you treated us like this? Your father and I have been anxiously searching for you." NIV (Luke 2:48) Mary recognized Joseph as Jesus' father on earth. But in their exchange, Jesus asked his mother, "Why were you searching for me? Didn't you know I had to be in my Father's house?" Mary and his earthly dad were worried about him, but Jesus was about the work of his Heavenly Father in the temple.

The Scripture goes on to let us know that Jesus returned home with his parents and he was obedient to them. However, his mother treasured the things that occurred in her heart, while Jesus continued to grow in wisdom, in stature, and in favor with God and with men. Joseph, the dad who raised Jesus, had one of the most challenging jobs of all times; he had the responsibility of being a righteous example before the Lord of Glory every day of his life while he was here on earth as Emmanuel – "God with us." Dads, while Joseph had the great and awesome challenge of parenting the Lord of Glory here on earth, he never relinquished his God-given righteous authority. Fathers, in particular, are instructed in Scripture to raise our children in the discipline and instruction of the Lord; and Joseph never stopped being that type of dad.

Lessons Learned from the Life of Joseph:

1. **God calls dads to demonstrate righteous character before their family.**
2. **God expects dads to seek out righteous solutions.**
3. **Dads, it is God's responsibility to produce righteous outcomes.**
4. **Dads, your obedience to God's word will lead you into righteous pathways.**
5. **Dads, your righteous response will impact your family's spiritual growth.**
6. **Dads, maintain your God-given righteous authority in your family.**

CHAPTER XVIII

Lessons Learned from Jairus —
The Father of One Little Girl
(Luke 8:41-56; Mark 5:22-43)

Fathers who raise sons most often do so with pride knowing that their sons will carry on the family name. Fathers who raise sons share with them things they learned from their fathers about manhood and becoming a man. It is an awesome responsibility to raise a boy to become a man. It's my belief that you have to be a father who is raising or has raised a son to fully grasp the magnitude of the responsibility of raising a son into manhood. This is not to say that single mothers cannot raise sons into manhood, but there is a difference when it comes to fathers and their sons. However, for fathers who raise daughters, there is a whole other set of experiences. Raising sons is about their responsibility, but raising daughters is about your heart. Fathers become dads when they raise daughters because daughters touch fathers in places of the heart. Daughters for some reason have a special place in the heart of a dad. Daughters have the ability to bring dads to their knees; every instinct and emotion that a father possesses can be triggered by his love for his daughter and his daughter's love for him. It is not a matter of quantity, in other words, fathers don't love their daughters more than they love their sons, but it's different. Daughters trigger those instinctive attributes in the nature of their dads, and they bring out those attributes that rarely are thought of when defining manhood. However, it is these attributes that daughters bring out of their dads that uniquely define the father-daughter relationship.

Jairus, the ruler of the synagogue in Capernaum, was defined for us not by his administrative work at the synagogue, but by his relationship with his daughter. The gospel writers of Mark and Luke provide us with a sneak peek into the heart of a dad through the life experience of Jairus and his daughter. During the earthly ministry of Jesus, he spent quite a bit of time in and around the Sea of Galilee, and the story of Jairus and his daughter takes place as Jesus crossed over the sea, or lake as some call it, and he was welcomed by the crowd for they were expecting him. It was in that crowd of people that the story of Jairus and his daughter unfolds. The interesting thing about crowds is that you never know who might show up. This crowd had at least two people from different paths of life that converged at one moment in time. In this crowd there was Jairus, who was considered somebody important; he was the ruler of the synagogue, which was the center of Jewish religious worship. According to Luke's account, Jairus had only one daughter, who was 12 years old, and she was dying. Also in that welcoming crowd was an unnamed woman who had been sick with an issue of blood for 12 years and could not be made well, although she had seen many physicians throughout her life. Jairus will have a defining moment as these two lives converge in this crowd that gathered to welcome Jesus.

The story is one of two roads intersecting for the same purpose after 12 years on different paths. Jewish synagogue officials were not necessarily believers in Jesus as their Messiah, although they did believe in the miracles of God and his ability to do the miraculous. Jairus no doubt had heard about the miracles done by the Lord Jesus in the area; in fact, this story is in the middle of a series of miraculous events that Mark records in his gospel. Jairus was in the crowd, like so many others, anticipating Jesus' return to their shore so that he could inquire of him and make him aware of his daughter's condition, in hopes that Jesus would have compassion for her and come to his house and heal her of the sickness that was taking away her life at such a young age. Mark says that when Jairus saw Jesus, he fell at his feet and pleaded earnestly with him, saying, "My little daughter is dying. Please come and put your hands on her so that she will be healed and live." Jairus believed if Jesus touched his daughter she would live. The Scripture says that Jesus went with him and a large crowd followed and pressed around him. It was in that pressing around him that the second road intersected with Jairus' road to his daughter's healing.

Within the crowd that was pressing around Jesus was a woman who had been subject to uncontrollable bleeding for 12 years. This woman had suffered a great deal; she had been under the care of many doctors over the years and she spent all that she had trying to be made well. However, instead of getting better with all of this care, her condition continued to worsen. When she heard that Jesus was there she came up behind him. I suspect that she came up behind him because her issue of blood would have made her unclean in his sight and in the eyes of those in the crowd, and she would have had to declare that she was unclean so that people would keep their distance. So the woman decided if she could come up from behind him and just touch the hem or tassels of his garment she would be healed. Luke's account provides clarity that Mark's account leaves out; Luke includes that when the woman touched the edge of his garment her bleeding immediately stopped. Jesus then asked the question, "Who touched me?" His disciple Peter said, "Master, the people are crowding and pressing against you." But Jesus said, "Someone touched me; I know that power has gone out from me." When the woman realized that she could no longer go unnoticed, she came trembling and fell at Jesus' feet in the presence of all the people, and she told why she had touched him and how she had been instantly healed. Then he said to her, "Daughter, your faith has healed you. Go in peace." Lest you miss this observation, let me point out that this woman was an interruption to Jairus' problem. This woman was elevated from the back of the crowd to the front; this woman was a nobody who by faith became a somebody. Today we know of her and we learn from her because of her faith.

The woman with the issue of blood believed that if she could just touch the hem or tassels of Jesus' garment she would be made well; while at the same time Jairus believed that if Jesus could just touch his daughter she would be made well. Both believed that Jesus had the ability to handle their situation and bring about healing. Dads have to remember that regardless of their status in life there are some things that must be and can only be accomplished through faith in God. Nothing Jairus did in life or in his work in the synagogue prepared him for his daughter being sick and at the point of death. Jairus was apparently a wealthy man due to his occupation and the fact that he had a house that was large enough for a crowd to gather to mourn the death of his little girl. However, his status or his means could not affect his daughter's condition. There was only one thing that could affect his daughter's condition and that was the love of Jesus Christ in response to his faith. Our fathers have to have faith not only for themselves, but dads must have faith for their children as well. Dads, we have to pray for our children not just because we want the best for them, but we have to pray for them because there are times when they don't know how to pray or can't pray for themselves.

This story of Jairus' daughter and the woman with the issue of blood teaches us that in spite of the crowds and the billions of requests and people pressing against God, as it were, God's omnipotence is never challenged and is always ready and able to respond to those who come to him in faith. The woman with the issue of blood and Jairus' daughter would both come out of the shadows and become people for us to learn from.

Jairus came to Jesus in faith, believing that Jesus could heal his daughter, but as they were on their way to his house Jesus was interrupted by the woman with the issue of blood and while he took time to address her 12-year illness, Jairus is brought the news that his daughter has died. The Scripture says, While Jesus was still speaking, (that is, speaking to the woman) some men came from the house of Jairus, the synagogue ruler. "Your daughter is dead, "they said. "Why bother the teacher anymore?" As a father, I can only imagine what went through Jairus' mind upon hearing them say that "Your daughter is dead." Here he was on the way to his house with the one who could do something about her condition and he gets distracted by a poor woman with no status, with no children, and his daughter dies. But according to both Mark and Luke's account, Jesus immediately said to Jairus, "Don't be afraid; just believe." Luke adds, "And she will be healed." Jesus knew the natural inclination that Jairus would have after receiving such horrible news. Dads, sometimes circumstances can get so bad that even men with the greatest faith will fall victim to fear. It is in those moments that we have to remember that God has not given us the spirit of fear; but of power, and love and of a sound mind. NKJV (2 Timothy 1:7)

Within Jesus' exhortation to Jairus is a deep theological truth. Leon Morris in his commentary on Luke says that the tense in which Jesus addressed Jairus' internal fears is in what is called the "aorist tense" in the Greek language in which the New Testament was written. The "aorist tense" conveys the idea of doing something in the pass that has continuous results or outcomes. In its basic form, Jesus was telling Jairus to "keep on believing."[10]One might say you started believing now keep on believing, don't stop believing. Like Jairus, sometimes our circumstances can go from bad to worse, but that does not change, nor does it alter God's ability to handle our circumstances. In fact, sometimes the worse our circumstances become the more they exemplify the power of God. Oftentimes when our circumstances are within the realm of human possibility to handle, we work things out ourselves and then attribute the credit to ourselves or even worse we say what God did special for us, when, in fact, we were pulling strings and manipulating the situation for our desired outcome. Dads, when God allows our circumstances to get to the point where there is nothing we can possibly do to affect the situation, it is at that point that Jesus says, as he said to Jairus, "Don't be afraid; just believe." Dads, you and I have to be the ones in our families who keep on believing; our family's faith is fueled by the faith that they see in us.

Like Jairus' situation with his daughter, sometimes there are interruptions on the way to a miraculous breakthrough. The woman with the issue of blood was an interruption, the messenger who brought the news that his only child had died was an interruption, the crowd of mourners was an interruption, but these interruptions did not nor could they prevent the power of God from changing the circumstances in which Jairus found himself. Dads, we have to remember that Jesus Christ is the author and the finisher of our faith, according to the Scriptures. Dads, you and I must possess full and complete faith in the fact that there is nothing that is too hard for God. When faced with difficult circumstances, we must ask and answer the question that God asked Abraham after informing him that his wife Sarah, who was 90 years old and barren, was going to have a son. The Lord asked Abraham, "Is anything too difficult for the Lord?" NASB (Genesis 18:14) You and I have to answer that question.

You and I have to answer the question that God asked Moses when the children of Israel complained that God was miraculously feeding them daily with manna during their wilderness journey; having miraculously escaped the hand of Pharaoh by the miraculous crossing of the Red Sea. Moses asked God how was he to find enough meat to feed more than 600,000 people, not counting women and children. God's response to Moses was "Is the Lord's arm too short?" NIV (Numbers 11:23) Although God desired to provide his children with their daily portion of manna, the question before him was how could he provide them with meat instead? The Scripture says that not only could God provide enough meat for them to eat, but God caused a wind to blow in quail from the ocean that stacked up about three feet deep for the space of a full day's walk. However, because they did not believe, God caused them to become sick as the quail were still in their teeth. (Numbers 11)

When it comes to our faith in God the question is always the same: "Is anything too hard for the Lord?" The Lord said to Jeremiah the prophet, "I am the Lord, the God of all mankind. Is anything too hard for me?" NIV (Jeremiah 32:27) Jesus illustrates the value of continued faith in him with his disciples after his resurrection. Jesus had appeared to the disciples individually and in small groups, but, for the most part, he discontinued performing the types of miracles that he did prior to his crucifixion. Thus, his disciples decided they would go back to doing the things they did prior to the start of his ministry, so they went fishing. The disciples had fished all night and caught nothing, but when morning came, Jesus called out to these experienced fishermen and asked, "Friends, haven't you any fish?" They replied, "No." Jesus told them to cast their nets on the right side of their boat and they would find some fish. When they believed him and did as he told them, their nets were full with 153 large fish. This was the second occasion that Jesus had instructed the disciples in the fine art of catching fish. On the first occasion, pre-crucifixion, they caught so many fish that their nets began to break. Again, the question is always the same: "Is anything too hard for the Lord?"

The Scripture says, "In the beginning was the Word, and the Word was with God and the Word was God. He was with God in the beginning. Through him all things were made; without him nothing was made that has been made." "... He was in the world, and though the world was made through him, the world did not recognize him." NIV (John 1:1-10) Surely the one who made the world and all that is in it knew where the fish were, and, figuratively speaking, he knows where the fish are in our lives.

Jairus' need for his daughter to be healed was interrupted, but the interruptions did not prevent the Lord from responding. When Jesus arrived at Jairus' home, he put everyone out with the exception of his three closest disciples, Peter, James and John, and her parents before doing anything. Dads, some circumstances are so difficult that it is best to limit your circle to a small number of people of faith. Your faith must remain focused in times of difficulty and, more often than not, the crowds are nothing more than a distraction. The crowd laughed at Jesus when he said the child was not dead but asleep; crowds have a tendency to be wrong and, again, you never know who's in the crowd. Unfortunately, in today's world, everyone wants to be with the crowd. I have found that some of God's most amazing work is done away from the crowds. I am reminded of Psalm 91: 1-2: "He who dwells in the secret place of the Most High shall abide under the shadow of the Almighty." I will say of the Lord, "He is my refuge and my fortress; My God, in Him I will trust." [11] NKJV Great things happen in the secret place of the Most High.

Dads, the Scripture says Jesus called the little girl "Talitha koum!" (which means "Little girl, I say to you, get up!"). Immediately the little girl stood up and walked around to the amazement of those in his house. The Bible says unless we become like little children, we will never enter the kingdom of heaven. It says that we have to humble ourselves like little children. In other words, we have to learn to do what little children do naturally, which is to trust. The woman with the issue of blood became like a child and came to Jesus on her knees, trusting him to heal her of her illness. Jairus had to become like a child and trust without fear. When Jesus exhorted Jairus not to be afraid, he was saying to this leader of the synagogue become like your little daughter and trust me. When our circumstances get beyond our ability to handle or affect the outcome, we have to exercise our faith in the Lord Jesus Christ and the promises of His Word. Dads, remember the question is always the same: "Is there anything too hard for the Lord?" Jairus teaches us that there is nothing that is too hard for the Lord.

Lessons Learned from Jairus:

1. **Dads, it is not what you do that defines who you are; it is what you believe that defines who you are.**
2. **Faith in God can accomplish for you what wealth, status and prestige could never allow you to accomplish.**

3. Dads have to maintain faith, not just for themselves, but for their family as well.

4. God's omnipotence is never challenged by life's interruptions and is always capable of responding to those who call upon him in faith believing.

5. Dads, your family's faith is fueled by your continuous belief and trust in God.

6. When you find yourself in difficult circumstances only allow a small number of people of faith in your inner circle.

7. Jairus teaches us that we must forever ask and answer the question: "Is there anything too hard for the Lord?"

CHAPTER XIX

Lessons Learned from —
The Father of the Prodigal Son (Luke 15:11-31)

Parables are unique methods of storytelling employed by those who teach to explain or reveal hard to understand spiritual truths. They utilize familiar earthly items to explain unfamiliar and hard to understand spiritual truths. Jesus used parables in his ministry. He was the master at using parables to teach his disciples and the masses. Luke's gospel records a series of parables that Jesus used to teach his disciples and the masses that followed him. The most famous of his parables are arguably "The Good Samaritan" and "The Parable of the Lost Son."

On this occasion Jesus had just finished teaching his followers a lesson on the cost of discipleship, the importance of counting up the cost to finish something before you start the building process. He also taught the lesson of the lack of value that salt has when it loses its flavor; when he was approached by a group of tax collectors and those whom the Scripture says were sinners and a group of religious Pharisees and scribes who complained that "this Man receives sinners and eats with them." The religious people were complaining that Jesus received those who were not religious. The last time I checked, the Scripture says, "For the Son of Man has come to seek and to save that which was lost." NIV (Luke 19:10) However, these religious leaders did not see things that way. So Jesus employed the use of three parables to address their concerns about with whom he was associating: "The Lost Sheep," "The Lost Coin" and "The Lost Son." Regarding the lost sheep, Jesus said if a man had 100 sheep and he lost one wouldn't he leave the 99 and go after the one that has strayed and become lost. Regarding the lost coin, he said if a woman had 10 silver coins and she lost one in her house would she not sweep the house clean until she found the one that was lost, and when she found it, wouldn't she call her friends to rejoice with her over the one coin that was lost that is now found. Then there was the man with the lost son; how much more valuable is the lost son who is found?

The story of the prodigal son has always fascinated me for many different reasons; I think primarily because at some juncture in my life I have seen glimpses of myself in all three characters of the story. We are told that: "A certain man had two sons. And the younger of them said to his father, 'Father, give me the portion of goods that falls to me.' So he divided to him his livelihood. And not many days after, the younger son gathered all together, journeyed to a far country, and there wasted his possessions with prodigal living. But when he had spent all, there arose a severe famine in that land, and he began to be in want." This parable is what I call a preacher's paradise; if a minister can't preach this text, he is in the wrong profession. It has all the elements for a great Sunday morning sermon. Here we have a father with two sons and the younger son decides that he cannot wait for his father to die to receive his inheritance so he wants his portion now. This is so typical of the foolishness of youth. This young man, like many young men today, could not see the value in waiting. There are some things that we give our children too soon, and this was one of them.

According to Jewish law, the inheritance was to be distributed in portions and the elder son would receive a double portion of the inheritance and the younger son would receive one third the amount. (Deut. 21:17) Although the inheritance could be given prior to one's death, the interest income would remain with the original donor until his death. However, the younger son wasted no time taking his portion and all that he had and gathered it up for his journey; he had no intentions of returning for anything. The Scripture is clear when it says that he went to a far country, his intent was clear. I think when we get to the older brother's story, we may get a glimpse into why the younger brother went so far away. As Jesus is telling this parable, he said that this son went to this far country and when he got there he wasted his possessions with "prodigal living." He spent his money and resources freely, recklessly, and wastefully on extravagance; his older brother even said that he wasted his money on prostitutes.

The younger son suddenly found himself in a precarious dilemma; all of his inheritance had quickly drained and there arose a severe famine in that country and he began to starve. In times of famine there are ancillary consequences attached to the lack of food, such as the lack of work and means of income generation. People often times become more self-centered and less willing to share the little that they have with others. This young son found himself on the bottom looking for a way up. He did what no Jewish man would do; he went and joined himself to a citizen of that country, who sent him into his fields to feed the swine. According to Jewish law, swine were unclean and not to be eaten or their carcass touched. (Lev.11:7) Jewish people would have nothing to do with swine and here this young son is not only feeding them, but Jesus said that this son had fallen so low that he would have gladly filled himself with the pods that the swine ate because no one would give him anything. Times were tough for everyone, however, it could have been because of the way this young man lived in that country with his inheritance that no one was willing to help him. I suspect that in his youthful judgment or lack thereof he was not the most humble or respectful guest of that country. His demand for his inheritance lets us know that he was impatient and selfish, and the money no doubt made him even more of what he already was – impatient, selfish and disrespectful.

However, something happened to this young man as he discovered how low he had fallen. Here he was a young Jewish man waddling around in a pig pen, feeding pigs, ready to eat what pigs ate, and he had a father in a distance country who was rich with servants, houses and land of his own. This son was like so many of us, we take off on our own without direction in life and we end up in places that we cannot stay, places we never believed we would be, doing things we never imagined we would do, when we have a father in heaven who says, "For every beast of the forest is Mine, And the cattle on a thousand hills... If I were hungry, I would not tell you; For the world is Mine, and all its fullness." NKJV (Psalm 50:10; 12) Yet we find ourselves like this "prodigal son," living with pigs, sleeping with pigs, eating with pigs, but like this "prodigal son" we have to remember that we have a father who is rich in glory and can supply all our needs. The apostle Paul said, "And my God shall supply all your needs according to His riches in glory by Christ Jesus." NKJV (Philippians 4:19)

When this young son came to himself, when he regained his perspective and remembered whose he was, he didn't let how far he had fallen keep him from reclaiming who he was. Dads, one of the reasons we have to remain strong is so that when our sons and daughters come to themselves after life has beaten them down they have some place to come back to that they can call home; even if just for a little while. The younger son realized that he had fallen as low as he could fall short of death, and he had a father who could immediately resolve his dilemma of starvation and wantonness. The young son said to himself, "How many of my father's hired servants have bread enough to spare, and I perish with hunger! I will arise and go to my father, and will say to him,'Father, I have sinned against heaven and before you, and I am no longer worthy to be called your son. Make me like one of your hired servants.'" NKJV (Luke 15:17-19) Listen to the words of this son; let them ring in your mind for just a minute, "Father, I have sinned." These words would make any father open his arms to his son or daughter, but to God they are some of the sweetest words He hears you and I say to him.

So as the young son made his way back to his father's house, he prepared his mind for the conversation that he would have with his dad so that his dad would receive him back, if not as his son, at least as a servant, which far exceeded where he had fallen. However, before he could get the words out of his mouth, his dad, who had been looking for him, saw him coming from a great distance and, overwhelmed with compassion, ran to him and the Scripture says that he threw his arms around his son's neck and kissed him. Dads, this was a father who was looking forward with great expectations to his son's return. This was a dad who no doubt missed the relationship that he enjoyed with his son. Real parenting is an interesting experience; parents who love their children love having them around. Even when it comes time to let them go out on their own, it is overwhelming joy when they return. I am reminded of the many times that our children have gone off to college or on some independent trip; it brings me great joy when my wife and I go to the airport and see them for the first time as they come through the crowd of travelers. I always like to position myself so that I can see them coming from a distance so I can see how much they have changed since being away. This father was no different, he was positioned to see his son coming from a distance. I suggest that if you have a "prodigal child" never stop expecting him or her to come to themselves and to return; this father didn't.

What this father did is an example for all of us fathers of how we should consider responding to our returning prodigal. This dad told his household servants, "Bring out the best robe and put it on him, and put a ring on his hand and sandals on his feet. And bring the fatted calf here and kill it, and let us eat and be merry; for this my son was dead and is alive again; he was lost and is found." NKJV (Luke 15:22-24) George Arthur Buttrick, in his exposition of these verses, provides us with an insightful commentary on the meaning of each of the father's actions. Buttrick says the **kiss** that the father bestowed upon his son was one of tenderness because of the shameful appearance of his son and his son's need to know that his father still loved him as much as, if not more than, he did before he became lost. According to Buttrick, when the father told his servants to bring the items for his son the idea behind the term bring was to "bring quickly" the requested items because not a minute could be wasted in restoring this son to his rightful place in the family. "**The best** robe" was reserved for honored guest and the father called for the "the best robe" to be brought and put on his son. The father's act of restoration was like God's act of restoration – there is no second best; when God restores us he gives us his best. The **ring** was a sign of ownership and authority; this son was still an heir. Although he had spent his portion of his inheritance he was still entitled to all other things that came with his father's name and rebuilding a life was now possible and in order. The **sandals** for his feet were the token of son-ship. Slaves went without shoes for their feet, but sons had shoes. Buttrick reminds his readers of the old Negro spiritual and says that it has caught both the joy and the pathos of that gift: "All o' God's children got shoes. When I get to heaven I'm going to put on my shoes, I'm going to walk all over God's heaven." Buttrick suggest that when the father said that his son who was dead is now alive was equating his lost condition to being dead. He reminds us that the Scripture says, "He that hears my word...is passed from death unto life." NASB (John 5:24) Thus he equates being found to being alive. What Buttrick suggest is that the father's love for his son restored the son's life. Dads, you and I, if we love our children unconditionally, we have the power to restore them to life when they are dead as this prodigal son's father said; "for this my son was dead and is alive again." They prepared the **fatted calf** and they celebrated the return of the young son. This calf had been prepared from its birth for such a time as this, and, like our Lord Jesus, this calf was sacrificed for the restoration of this lost son.[12]

One of the fascinating things about the Bible is that it does not leave out nor does it sugarcoat inappropriate behavior or inappropriate responses because they may cause someone to be embarrassed or shamed by their revelation. And so Jesus does not leave out the older brother's response to all this joy and celebratory behavior. Earlier I said that we might discover why the young son prematurely demanded his inheritance and left and I suspect that the older brother's actions will give us some insight into that decision. As Jesus was telling the story of this family he said that the older brother was in the field, which leads me to believe that the older brother was in the field working for his living. The younger brother had left and went out and spent his money on prodigal living while the older brother stayed home and worked the fields. I suspect that at least one of the young son's reasons for leaving had something to do with the responsibilities and work that his father had placed upon him and his brother. No one can blame the father for teaching his sons responsibility through work, but it seems as though the older son equated his earning a living with earning his father's love. Jesus said that when the servants told the older son what his father was doing for his younger brother who had returned the older son became angry a would not participate in the celebration.

When the father heard that his older son was angry and refused to join the celebration he went out to his son and pleaded with him to come. This reminds me so much of how our Heavenly Father goes out looking for us and pleads with us and invites us to come and join the celebration of life. But the older son said, "Lo all these many years I have been serving you; I never transgressed your commandment at any time; and yet you never gave me a young goat that I might make merry with my friends. But soon as this son of yours came, who has devoured your livelihood with harlots; you killed the fatted calf for him." NKJV (Luke 15:29-30) The older son believed that his righteousness should have merited him at least a young goat; he didn't ask for a fatten calf, he would have settled for a young goat. Many times we think just like the older son, we think that our own conjured up acts of righteousness should merit favor with our Heavenly Father like they often do with men. The father's response was the epitome of unconditional love; he said, "Son you are always with me, and **all** that I have is yours. It was right that we should make merry and be glad, for **your brother** was dead and is alive again, and was lost and is found." NKJV (Luke 15:31-32)

Let's break down what the father was saying to his son. First of all, the older son did not want to reclaim the younger son; he said to his father "this son of yours." He wanted to disassociate himself from his brother because of how his brother lived. This brother could no more disassociate himself from his brother than I could from my brother or you could from your brother. It's been said that the Christian church is the only army that kills its wounded. Christian brothers and sisters fall all the time, some even stray away from the faith, but when they return we are to restore them in the spirit of gentleness less we ourselves be overtaken in our own temptations. The Apostle Paul said, "Brothers, if someone is caught in a sin, you who are spiritual should restore him gently. But watch yourself, or you also may be tempted. Carry each other's burdens, and in this way you will fulfill the law of Christ. If anyone thinks he is something when he is nothing, he deceives himself." NIV (Galatians 6:1-3) The father was saying to his older son, your brother got what was rightfully his when he left with his portion of the inheritance; your portion is still completely secured. We, like the older brother, oftentimes think that because someone else receives a blessing that somehow our blessing is going to be affected. However, that is so far from the truth; what God has for you is for you and what God has for your brother or sister is for them. The father was saying that their rejoicing over the younger son who was lost and was now found in no way affected the love he had for his older son.

When I started this chapter, I said to you that I could identify with all three of the characters in this parable. I have been the younger son who took all that he had and went off to a far and distant land and sometimes spent money and family resources foolishly and wastefully. In 1977, after completing my basic training in the Ohio Army National Guard, I returned home for a few weeks during my transition back into civilian life. While there I made the mistake of saying a little too much about one of my younger sibling's behavior, and I was quickly reminded that I was not paying any bills in that house and needed to keep my opinions to myself. However, for me, as a young man not yet fully matured in my Christian faith, keeping my opinions to myself was not an option. The next morning I loaded up my car and I left home and have been on my own ever since.

I have been the father who restored a returning child. On more than one occasion I have been the father watching and waiting for a returning child. Sometimes they were expected to return and on other occasions particularly with our son there were times when we hoped he would return. One of your more difficult times as a parent is when it's gone bad and you have to mend the relationship. When trust between parent and child has been broken, you have to repair the trust. There are times when you feel like you are walking on eggshells to keep things in balance lest the child leaves again and the pain of loss starts all over again. I have found that the best way for me to get pass the pain and not to walk on eggshells was to get right back into the saddle of parenting. In other words, because the child returned and you may be churning inside, don't give up your parental authority, even if it means the child leaves again. I'll watch and wait at the doorway as the prodigal's father did, but, as he did, I will not relinquish my parental authority. When children leave and return, although you need to show them your overwhelming unconditional love and support, they still need to know that you are the parent and they are the child. The prodigal's dad did that with his authoritative commands to his servants to prepare the celebration for his son who had returned. He also did it with the older son by reminding him that his inheritance was still completely intact.

Of these three characters, I have been most like the older son. In 1980, four years after finishing high school, I realized that my life had not gained the traction that I had hoped for at that point in my life. This fact was made clear to me when a friend of mine, a young lady who I attended grade school with, began interning at the TV station where I worked. She was in her senior year of college at Ohio State University while I was a mere freshman, although we finished high school the same year. How does that happen? I had been on my own for three years and I was working more than going to school. When I began training her to do my job I decided to get serious about my life's calling and move to Dallas to begin my formal theological training and education.

I truly left all that I had to do this good work of obtaining a theological education to prepare myself for serving humanity. When I moved to Dallas I had no place to live, I had no job, I had no personal transportation and I knew only one person who lived in Dallas and that was Larry Freeman, who is one of the best human beings I know. In fact, I don't think I know a more humble person than Larry. Larry told me I could stay where he was staying, but, unfortunately, by the time I arrived, things had changed and Larry had to move because the guy he was staying with had gotten engaged to be married. Thus, Larry and I both were without a place to live. Fortunately, Larry found another seminary student who let us sleep on the floor of his one room apartment, but he, too, was engaged, so once again we had to quickly find a new place to live. Larry and I were fortunate to find a very reasonable but roach infested place not far from Dallas Seminary's campus, but, once again, we found ourselves sleeping on the floor.

It was in this setting that the elder brother tendencies began to show up in my life. I had an older brother who lived a completely different lifestyle than his little brother – the Bible college student who was preparing to save the world. The reality was that I was studying the Bible and theology seven days a week while barely surviving on a couple of part-time jobs, sleeping on floors, driving a beat up old broken down pickup that I bought on the way to Dallas, eating beans and hot dogs or canned soup while my brother was living a life of plenty. It was during those years when my brother had plenty to share with friends and family that it appeared to me that he was the one being embraced by the family and I was the one being shunned. My brother once told me that I was the kind of person who would endure the hardships of life if I thought the end would be better, and he was right. However, I was like the prodigal's elder brother in the sense that I believed that my life's choices should have endeared my family and friends to me much more than they were endeared to my brother's life. But, like the prodigal's brother, I did not realize at the time that my brother needed my family's love as much if not more than I needed their love. I had the love of new family and friends through my relationship with the Lord Jesus Christ. I was receiving a formal education that would launch me into a career; I had a mission and purpose in my life; I had eternal assurance of my relationship with my Heavenly Father, all of which my brother had yet to evidence. However, before his passing, he put his faith in Christ, and I will see him again someday when I meet him in heaven.

Like the prodigal son's brother, everything my Father in heaven owns has been at my disposal all these years; I have a promise of an inheritance; the Scripture says we are heirs of God and joint heirs with Jesus Christ. While I was concerned about the love and affection shown my brother, I forgot to remember that he was my brother, and he deserved as much of our family's love as any other sibling regardless of his life choices. What I learned from the prodigal son's father is that there are no good sons and bad sons; when it comes to a father's love, there are only sons and daughters. You may have a son or daughter who makes bad choices in life, as they sometimes do, but you and I need to watch for them coming home because so often they feel the way the prodigal son felt toward his father: shame, guilt, embarrassment, failure, disgrace, unworthiness, and most of all unloved. Dads, your children need to know, more than anything else, that you, more than anyone else, love them even when they fall to their deepest depths in life; especially when they fall. Your love can be and often times is their lifeline to salvation.

Lessons Learned from the Father of the Prodigal Son:

1. Dads who give their children unrestricted inheritances often times do more harm than good.
2. Dads, it is imperative that our children believe they can always come home.
3. Never give up your expectations for children to come to themselves and return home.

4. Dads, when your prodigal child returns, do not waste a minute before restoring your child to his or her rightful place within the family.

5. When a father responds with unconditional love, it will restore a prodigal child.

6. Dads are the spiritual leaders in the family as it pertains to restoration of relationships.

7. Dads, in the process of restoration, never relinquish your parental authority for fear of your children leaving again.

8. All that my Father in heaven owns is at my disposal because I am his child.

9. There is no such thing as good sons and daughters and bad sons and daughters; there are simply sons and daughters who make good and bad choices.

10. If your children have fallen to the deepest depths in life, they need to be able to look up and still see their father's love for them, which may be their only lifeline to salvation.

PART THREE

Parenting Lessons Learned through Biblical Relationships

CHAPTER XX

Lessons Learned from God the Father
God's Relationship with His Children —
Genesis 1:1-26

When you think about God's relationship with His children, it is almost incomprehensible to think that He would actually have a relationship with mankind in our current state. However, His word – the Bible – says He does, and those of us who are people of faith in the truthfulness of the Bible believe that He does have a relationship with His children. As I began to think about the nature of the relationship that God has with His children, I pondered how I would tell a condensed version of the story. As I understand the Bible, the entire book is about the revelation of Jesus Christ and His relationship with His children, so I concluded the best way to look at this relationship is through the prism of His own words.

For example, in Genesis 1:26-28, God describes how we were created which provides great insight into how we, as His children, are viewed by Him. The Bible says,

> Then God said, "Let Us make man in Our image, according to Our likeness; and let them rule over the fish of the sea and over the birds of the sky and over the cattle and over every creeping thing that creeps on the earth." And God created man in His own image, in the image of God He created

> him; male and female He created them. And God
> blessed them; and God said to them, "Be fruitful
> and multiply, and fill the earth,…" NASB

So I begin with the premise that man, both male and female, was created by God in His image and given dominion in the earth. When we think about the creative act of God, there is a clear distinction between the creation of the earth and all of its component parts and the creation of mankind.

In the creation of the earth and its component parts God said, "Let there be" and it was so; "Let there be light," and there was light; "Let there be an expanse between the waters to separate water from water,"…. And it was so. God said, "Let the waters under the sky be gathered to one place and let dry ground appear." And it was so. Then God said, "Let the land produce vegetation: seed-bearing plants and trees on the land that bear fruit with seed in it, according to their various kinds." And it was so. And God said, "Let there be lights in the expanse of the sky to separate the day from the night, and let them serve as signs to mark seasons and days and years, and let them be lights in the expanse of the sky to give light on the earth." And it was so. And God said, "Let the water teem with living creatures, and let birds fly above the earth across the expanse of the sky." So God created the great creatures of the sea and every living and moving thing with which the water teams, according to their kind. And God saw that it was good. God endowed His creation with His divine blessing and commanded them to be fruitful and increase in number fill the water in the sea, and the birds were to increase and fill the earth. NIV (Genesis 1:9-21)

In God's final two creative acts He said, "Let the land produce living creatures according to their kind…" And it was so. And God saw that it was good. God's final creative act was the creation of mankind. Mankind's creation was uniquely different from the rest of creation. Whereas, all that was created up to this point was created by God addressing the earth and commanding an action to occur;

"Let there be." However, the creation of mankind demonstrates God's desire to engage in a relationship with His creation. It is a result of divine decree that man was created, "Let us make man in Our image, in Our likeness..." God's desire to have a relationship with mankind is evidenced by this fact that God created mankind in such a form that we share in His likeness in several ways. God breathed into mankind. God formed mankind and breathed into his nostrils the breath of life, and man became a living being. No other element of creation has that distinction. The psalmist says in Psalm 139:13-16:

> For you created my inmost being; you knit me together in my mother's womb. I praise you because I am fearfully and wonderfully made; your works are wonderful, I know that full well. My frame was not hidden from you when I was made in the secret place. When I was woven together in the depths of the earth, your eyes saw my unformed body. All the days ordained for me were written in your book before one of them came to be." NIV

The psalmist makes it abundantly clear that God knows us intimately from the inside out and there is, therefore, no where that we can go from Him and His knowledge of us. Because God formed us in His image He wants to relate to us as His children.

God wants to relate to His children in the image in which He created us, not in the essence of what we have become as a result of man's sin and the fall as recorded in Genesis 3. We are, therefore, instructed to put to death those things that belong to our earthly nature and put on those things that belong to Christ and the new nature that He gives us when we believed. The Apostle Paul spells this out in his writings in the letter to the Colossians 3:5-10:

> Put to death, therefore, whatever belongs to your earthly nature: sexual immorality, impurity, lust,

evil desires and greed, which is idolatry. Because of these, the wrath of God is coming. You used to walk in these ways in the life you once lived. But now you must rid yourself of all such things as these: anger, rage, malice, slander, and filthy language from your lips. Do not lie to each other, since you have taken off your old self with its practices and have put on the new self, which is being renewed in knowledge in the image of its Creator. NIV

In Ephesians 4:22-24 once again we are admonished to put off our old self, our former way of living and put on our new self, created to be like God in true righteousness and holiness. As dads, this is a key principle that we must engage; putting off the old and taking on the new.

In Romans 12:1-2 we dads are taught how to implement this principle idea of taking off the old and putting on the new. The Apostle Paul put it this way when he wrote: "I beseech you therefore brethren, by the mercies of God, that you present your bodies a living sacrifice, holy, acceptable unto God, which is your reasonable service. And be not conformed to this world; but be ye transformed by the renewing of your mind, that you may prove what is that good, and acceptable, and perfect, will of God." NKJV

Putting on the new self is about renewing your mind and having a heart that is given over to God. That's why Paul said present yourself as a living sacrifice holy acceptable to God. When dads get this part right most of the other parts of being a dad fall into place. That is what Paul means when he says "prove what is that good, and acceptable, and perfect, will of God." Dads, if you want your life to be in order so you can know how to be a good and righteous dad, get this part right first.

> *Biblical parenting takes spiritual discernment*

I have spoken extensively about being in God's image and

putting on this new self, but why is this important to me as a dad and how does one do what I am advocating? The reason it's important that we put on the new self or the new man, as it is called, is because to do what I am advocating and what I believe the Bible advocates one must have a change in one's life. The fact of the matter is to fully understand the things that I am advocating one must be changed. Biblical parenting takes spiritual discernment. When we operate with spiritual discernment God reveals to us the mysteries of His will and when we know and understand the mystery of His will we are then able to do what He says; not only in the arena of parenting and being good dads, but we are able to do His will in all other areas of our lives. In 1 Corinthians 1:18-25, Apostle Paul said the things of God are spiritual and they are spiritually discerned, and the man who is not spiritually aligned with God through Christ Jesus, to him these things of God are foolishness.

> For the message of the cross is foolishness to those who are perishing, but to us who are being saved it is the power of God. For it is written: I will destroy the wisdom of the wise; the intelligence of the intelligent I will frustrate. Where is the wise man? Where is the scholar? Where is the philosopher of this age? Has not God made foolish the wisdom of the world? For since in the wisdom of God the world through its wisdom did not know him, God was pleased through the foolishness of what was preached to save those who believe... Jews demand miraculous signs and Greeks (Gentiles) look for wisdom, but we preach Christ crucified; a stumbling block to Jews and foolishness to Gentiles, but to those whom God has called, both Jews and Greeks, (Gentiles) Christ the power of God and the wisdom of God. For the foolishness of God is wiser than man's wisdom, and the weakness of God, is stronger than man's strength. NIV

Paul goes on to say in 1 Corinthians 2:9-14 that the mystery of God, even the hidden wisdom which belongs to God has been ordained before the world for our glory. No one has seen it, no one has access to it except those to whom God has revealed it.

> However, as it is written: No eye has seen, no ear has heard, no mind has conceived what God has prepared for those who love him, but God has revealed it to us by His Spirit. The Spirit searches all things, even the deep things of God. For who among men knows the thoughts of a man except the man's spirit within him? In the same way no one knows the thoughts of God except the Spirit of God. We have not received the spirit of the world but the Spirit who is from God, that we may understand what God has freely given us. This is what we speak, not in words taught us by human wisdom but in words taught by the Spirit, expressing spiritual truths in spiritual words. The man without the Spirit does not accept the things that come from the Spirit of God, for they are foolishness to him, and he cannot understand them, because they are spiritually discerned... NIV

What I am saying to dads is if you want to be the kind of dad who practices biblical parenting, however that looks, it has to start with you being connected to the source of biblical wisdom. When you are connected to the source of wisdom parenting decisions take on a whole other dimension; it becomes a spiritual journey that comes with a road map. How often have we heard it said that parenting doesn't come with a guide? Well, let me suggest that the myth is not true, there is a guide to spiritual

Biblical parenting starts with being connected to the source of wisdom

parenting and the Bible provides us with that road map into the hidden mysteries of God's will which include how to parent our children. The key to unlocking the mystery of His will and discovering the path that God has prepared for us in parenting is being connected to Him through faith in Jesus Christ.

When we put our faith and trust in Jesus Christ our relationship with God enters into a whole new dimension. In the Gospel of John 1: 10-14, Apostle John writes these words regarding our new relationship with God:

> He was in the world, and though the world was made through Him, the world did not recognize him. He came to that which was his own, but his own did not receive him. Yet to all who received him, to those who believed in his name, he gave the right to become children of God – children born not of natural descent, nor of human decision or a husband's will, but born of God. The Word became flesh and made his dwelling among us. We have seen his glory, the glory of the One and Only, who came from the Father, full of grace and truth. NIV

Dads who want to practice biblical fatherhood have to know God and demonstrate His attributes before their children.

Those who believe in Jesus Christ the Son of God, He gives us the right and all of the privileges of son-ship which includes free access to the wisdom and all other resources of our Father. Paul says in Romans 8:14-17:

For as many as are led by the Spirit of God, they are the sons of God. For you have not received the spirit of bondage again to fear; but you have received the Spirit of adoption, whereby we cry Abba, Father. The Spirit itself bears witness with our spirit, that we are the children of God. And if children, then heirs; heirs of God, and joint-heirs with Christ; if so be that we suffer with him, that we may be also glorified together. NKJV

As a dad, my relationship to God the Father and His relationship to me is the supreme model for my relationship to my children. It is one of parent, protector, provider, and one who prescribes wisdom for living. John writes in 1 John 2:13: "I write to you, fathers, because you have known him who is from the beginning." NIV As a dad who wants to practice biblical fatherhood, I have to know God so that I can demonstrate His attributes before my children.

My daughters call me often for advice. I want to believe it's because they trust me to give them my best advice, and I believe they know that whatever we discuss, at the end of the conversation they will hear me say, "I love you." God's relationship with me is one in which I know that I can tell Him anything, no matter how personal, and at the end of my conversation with Him, through prayer, He always reminds me that He loves me. My goal is to emulate that attribute of God with my children. No matter how dark the situation, when God lets me know that He still loves me then I know that His light has illuminated my darkness.

A few years ago when the U.S. economy crashed and the company I work for went through what it called "transformation," life became very dark, as it were, for me and my family. I needed God's reassurance that the darkness of the situation had not changed His ability to be the Light of my life. Companies use words like "transformation, re-organization, restructuring, downsizing, right-sizing, re-alignment," or whatever they want to call it; at the end of the day, it's about people. When people's lives are turned upside down, they need assurance that help and hope is on the way. As a dad, when my life's circumstances got rocked after 30 years of commitment to an organization I needed to wrap my arms around something that was stronger than a 30-year career and 30 years of marriage with nearly 23 years of parenting. So in the midst of my darkest days, I sat down and began writing out the ways in which God had blessed me and my family over the previous 12 months in the midst of a global economic crisis. I counted 21 major blessings in the midst of an economic crisis and in the midst of an organizational "transformation." I then began writing out God's promises to His children as I set my goals for the year. I would like to share some of God's promises that I stood on during my darkest days.

God's Promises to Provide for His Children:

Proverbs 3:5-6
Trust in the Lord with all your heart, And lean not on your own understanding; In all your ways acknowledge Him, And He shall direct your paths. NKJV

2 Corinthians 9:8
And God is able to make all grace abound toward you; that ye, always having all sufficiency in all things, may abound to every good work: KJV

Philippians 4:19
But my God shall supply all your need according to his riches in glory by Christ Jesus. KJV

Psalm 37:25
I have been young, and now am old; yet have I not seen the righteous forsaken, nor his seed begging bread. KJV

Matthew 6:31-32

³¹Therefore take no thought, saying, What shall we eat? or, What shall we drink? or, Wherewithal shall we be clothed?

³²(For after all these things do the Gentiles seek,) for your heavenly Father knows that ye have need of all these things. KJV

Matthew 6:33

But seek first His kingdom and His righteousness, and all these things will be added to you. NASB

Matthew 7:11

If ye then, being evil, know how to give good gifts unto your children, how much more shall your Father which is in heaven give good things to them that ask him? KJV

Psalm 37:21

The wicked borrows and does not pay back, but the righteous is gracious and gives. NASB

Deuteronomy 28:12

The Lord will open for you His good storehouse, the heavens, to give rain to your land in its season and to bless all the work of your hand; and you shall lend to many nations, but you shall not borrow. NASB

Proverbs 3:9-10

Honor the Lord from your wealth and from the first of all your produce; So your barns will be filled with plenty and your vats will overflow with new wine. NASB

2 Corinthians 9:6-7

Now this I say, he who sows sparingly will also reap sparingly, and he who sows bountifully will also reap bountifully. Each one must do just as he has purposed in his heart, not grudgingly or under compulsion. NASB

Luke 6:38

Give, and it will be given to you. A good measure, pressed down, shaken together and running over, will be poured into your lap. For with the measure you use, it will be measured to you. NIV

Proverbs 11:25

The generous man will be prosperous, and he who waters will himself be watered. NASB

Psalm 37:4

Delight yourself in the Lord; And He will give you the desires of your heart. NASB

Joshua 1:8

This book of the law shall not depart from your mouth, but you shall meditate on it day and night, so that you may be careful to do according to all that is written in it; for then you will make your way prosperous, and then you will have success. NASB

Genesis 26:12

Then Isaac sowed in that land, and reaped in the same year a hundredfold; and the Lord blessed him. NKJV

Proverbs 10:22
The blessing of the Lord makes one rich, and He adds no sorrow with it. NKJV

Malachi 3:10
"Bring all the tithes into the storehouse, that there may be food in My house, and try Me now in this," Says the Lord of hosts, "If I will not open for you the windows of heaven And pour out for you such blessing that there will not be room enough to receive it. NKJV

Psalm 50:10-12
For every beast of the forest is Mine, the cattle on a thousand hills. I know every bird of the mountains, and everything that moves in the field is Mine. If I were hungry I would not tell you, for the world is Mine, and all it contains. NASB

1 Peter 5:6-7
Humble yourselves therefore under the mighty hand of God, that he may exalt you in due time: Casting all your care upon him for he careth for you. KJV

Romans 8:28
And we know that God causes all things to work together for good to those who love God, to those who are called according to His purpose. NASB

John 10:10
"...I am come that they might have life, and that they might have it more abundantly." NASB

Psalm 145:9
"The Lord is good to all: and his tender mercies are over all his works." NASB

Lamentations 3:22-23
"It is of the Lord's mercies that we are not consumed, because his compassions fail not. They are new every morning: great is thy faithfulness." KJV

Psalms 145:8
"The Lord is gracious, and full of compassion; slow to anger, and of great mercy." KJV

I posted these 25 scriptural promises on my bathroom mirror so that every morning and every evening I would be reminded of God's promises to provide for His children. When I came home at the end of a difficult day with questions of why or more specifically why me; God would always give me the same answer; so I can have a vehicle through which to demonstrate my love?

This reminds me of a time early in our marriage sometime after we had bought our first home and some emergency came up. I don't even remember what it was, but I know it was urgent and we didn't have the money to cover it so I went to my dad and asked if he could help us in our time of need. Although I don't remember the need, I will never forget what my dad did and said. My dad gave me his Gold Card and said, "Son when you need it is when I love to be able to give it to you." That's been well over 25 years but I never forgot the love that he showed that day. That day, my dad demonstrated the attributes of God by showing his unconditional love to Teresa and I. Every now and then I will stand there in my bathroom mirror and read aloud the promises of God to remind myself of just how much He loves us.

Lessons Learned from our Heavenly Father:

1. Biblical parenting requires spiritual discernment.
2. Biblical parenting starts with being connected to the source of wisdom.
3. Dads who practice biblical parenting have to know God and demonstrate His attributes before their children.
4. Dads who practice biblical parenting stand on the promises of God.

CHAPTER XXI

God the Father's Relationship with Jesus Christ His Only Begotten Son

As I began to generate the ideas for this book and think through what being a dad has meant to me, all the lessons learned, I shared my thoughts with my good friend the Rev. Lafayette Holland. He challenged me to think about one more relationship, that is the relationship between God the Father and Jesus Christ, His only begotten Son. Although this is the final chapter, it is by far the most intimidating and challenging of all. When it came to writing about lessons learned from the other biblical dads, some I approached thinking there's really not much there, but when I began researching and studying their lives more closely, I was amazed at how valuable they were and have been to my construct as a dad. Jesse comes to mind; on the surface, it did not appear to be much there, but he is a deep well of information and motivation. The prodigal son's dad is a powerful demonstrative model of a righteous dad. And who could forget Job? He went to 10 of his children's funerals and yet he remained steadfast with God.

However, as I begin to think about the God of creation and His relationship with His only begotten Son, my words fail me. Just now I am thinking about Jesus' words spoken on the cross: "My God, My God, why hast thou forsaken me." KJV (Matthew 27:46) I believe when Jesus spoke those words it was the moment at which he was experiencing what the Apostle Paul was referring to when he wrote: "God made him who had no sin to be sin for

us, so that in him we might become the righteousness of God."
NIV (2 Corinthians 5:21) This is not to say that God somehow
left Jesus at any point, but it is to say that Jesus suffered the loss of
that close fellowship because he was taking on our sin. Paul said in
verse 19 that "God was in Christ, reconciling the world to himself,
not imputing their trespasses unto them." NKJV God the Father
never stopped being eternally one with the Son. So as I write about
the relationship with God the Father and His only begotten Son,
it is these types of issues that make this not only intimidating, but
humbling beyond measure.

God the Father and Jesus Christ His only begotten Son share
in a relationship that is unique like no other father and son. Jesus
said in John 10:30 that He and the Father are one. What does that
mean? How does that look? These are all questions that theologians
have asked and attempted to answer for centuries. Let me simply
say without becoming too technical they share the same nature,
they share the same divine attributes. Theologians like to refer
to God the Father and God the Son and God the Holy Spirit as:
co-equal, co-existent and co-eternal. This is a relationship that no
human shares with any other human or with God.

I will attempt to describe the nature of their relationship as it
is recorded in Scripture. However, this will not be an exhaustive
description, but merely a gleaning of the surface. Dads should take
careful note to observe the nature of their relationship one with another
and seek to emulate its qualities in our relationships with our children.

Beloved

One of the first characteristics of the Father's relationship to
the Son is one of beloved: In Matthew 3:17, the gospel writer says,
"And lo a voice from heaven, saying, This is my beloved Son, in
whom I am well pleased." KJV Is your relationship to your children
characterized as beloved?

Eternal Bond

God the Father and Jesus Christ have an eternal bond. Jesus said to the Father in his priestly prayer in John 17:5: "And now, O Father, glorify Me together with Yourself, with the glory which I had with you before the world was." NKJV In John 1:1-2, the Scripture says, "In the beginning was the Word, and the Word was with God, and the Word was God. He was in the beginning with God..." NKJV (vs.14) "And the Word became flesh and dwelt among us, and we beheld His glory, the glory as of the only begotten of the Father, full of grace and truth." NKJV

As dads, we may not have an infinite history with our children, but we do have an infinite future with our children and we have the present. There will never be a time when your children, whether claimed or unclaimed, living or deceased, will not be your children. People who have lost children never stop acknowledging those children. I have an aunt who lost a child in a car accident when he was a teenager, and if you ask her today how many children she has, she will tell you that she has two living and one deceased. I have a very dear friend and pastor who lost a child when the child was very young, and if you ask he and his wife how many children do they have, they will tell you that they have four children, three living and one in heaven. Once you father a child, that child is connected to you for life and all eternity. Jesus asked the Father to glorify Him with the glory He had in eternity, we, likewise, should share in the glory of our children as they share in our glory.

Jesus said an interesting thing in His priestly prayer that we dads would do well to take hold. He said in John 17: 10 "And all Mine are Yours, and Yours are Mine, and I am glorified in them." NKJV Jesus was saying that everything and everyone that the Father had given to Him belonged to the Father and all that belonged to the Father belonged to the Son. This is a game changing truth for us dads. What it says in translation is that everything you and I have belongs to God the Father; He simply gave us stewardship over it. However, the flip side of that coin is that as it pertains to our own children all that we have really is theirs to share. Now I know that for some dads who will read this you will say "not in my house," but the reality is how many of us would not give all that we have to save one of our children? Often times I give my kids money or some other item and I truly do feel as though I am giving it to myself. Because, as for me and my house, we are one; whatever I have they have.

Ownership

Speaking of ownership, Jesus said in verse 11 of His priestly prayer: "Now I am no longer in the world, but these are in the world, and I come to You, Holy Father, keep through Your name those whom You have given Me, that they may be one as We are." NKJV Jesus asked His Father to allow us to have and share in the same type of relationship that He and His Father shared. As dads, we should desire that level of closeness with our children. This is not to say that we hold on to them and never let them discover themselves and the world in which we live, but we desire a close fellowship with them. One of my colleagues overheard me talking with one of my daughters on the phone and when our conversation concluded, they commented on how they perceived me to be as a dad from the half of the conversation they heard. They recognized that my daughter and I are close although we are thousands of miles apart. That's a closeness that I never want to lose.

Submission

How is it that God the Father and Jesus Christ His only begotten Son maintain their close fellowship, and how can us dads maintain a close fellowship with our children? God the Father and

Jesus Christ the Son clearly understand their distinct roles within the relationship. Dads, we must clearly understand our role in the relationship with our children. Jesus understood that although He and the Father were of the same essence, they had different functions. Theologians call it homogeneous, which means the same essence but different functions. Jesus' function was to be submissive to the will of God the Father. In His priestly prayer once again Jesus says, "I have given them Your word;... Sanctify them by Your truth. Your word is truth. As You have sent Me into the world, I also have sent them into the world. And for their sakes I sanctify Myself, that they also may be sanctified by the truth." NKJV (John 17:14-19) God the Father and Jesus Christ His Son had a relationship that worked because they understood their functions. In this instance, God the Father was the sender and Jesus the Son was the one who went. God the Father had the word, Jesus Christ the Son delivered the word; Jesus himself prayed that God the Father would sanctify, that is, to set us apart as He himself had been set apart. There are different roles and functions that make the relationship work. Paul said in his letter to the Ephesians, 6:1-4, that children are to obey their parents in the Lord, for this is right. Children are to honor their father and their mother, which is the first commandment with a promise: "That it may be well with you and you may live long on the earth." NKJV I take this to mean that there is a point where children need to just obey, period; no questions asked. However, as our children get older and become young adults and then adults, they don't have to obey their parents, but they do have to honor their parents. For example, now that our children are all young adults, I say they don't have to do everything we tell them to do at this point, but they do have to honor what we say, particularly since they are all receiving the benefits of being our children. My wife, their mother, would say as long as they accept benefits like money and other resources, they need to obey, regardless of their age. I don't necessarily disagree with her, but I think Paul makes a distinction.

However, the other side of maintaining a close relationship between dads and their children is the dad's role. In the same context of Ephesians 6 in verse 4, Paul said, "And you fathers, (dads) do not provoke your children to wrath, but bring them up in the training and admonition of the Lord." NKJV Dads, our role is to train and instruct our children in the Lord. In the Old Testament when God was laying out His Law to the children of Israel, He said this to the fathers after He gave them the greatest of all commandments:

> You shall love the Lord your God with all your heart, with all your soul, and with all your strength. And these words which I command you today shall be in your heart. You shall teach them diligently to your children, and shall talk of them when you sit in your house, when you walk by the way, when you lie down, and when you rise up. You shall bind them as a sign on your hand, and they shall be as frontlets between your eyes. You shall write them on the doorpost of your house and on your gates. NKJV (Deuteronomy 6:5-8)

Dads, our role is to be the spiritual heads of our homes, thus, our relationship with our children is deeply rooted in our spiritual development and transformation. Paul wrote in 1 Corinthians 11:3a: "Now I want you to realize that the head of every man is Christ." NIV Dads, as we desire our children to be submissive to us and to honor us, so also, God desires that we be submissive to and honor Him.

Holy Scripture says that the day is coming when Jesus Christ will have put all things under His feet, that is, in submission to Himself, the last of which is death; it is at that point that He will hand the Kingdom over to God the Father. If that's true and we believe it is, then dads we need to become submissive now and not wait.

Unconditional Eternal Love

In Jesus' priestly prayer, He expresses and reveals the nature of His relationship to the Father in the clearest of terms. Jesus said that God the Father loved Him before the creation of the world. Jesus prayed that those whom God has chosen would be so unified that the world would know that He was sent by God and that His love for us was the same kind of love that He himself received from the Father. (John 17:23-24) In John 15:9 Jesus said, "As the Father has loved me so have I loved you. Now remain in my love." NIV He went on to say, "Love each other as I have loved you." NIV (John 15:12) Dads, Christ tied our love to His love; we ought to love like He loved. He didn't love us because we were so lovely and lovable; in fact, Paul wrote in Romans 5:8 "But God demonstrated his own love for us in this; while we were still sinners, Christ died for us." NIV His love for us is like God's love for Him; eternal and unconditional. Jesus said in John 15:13; "Greater love has no one than this; that he lay down his life for his friends." NIV Dads, the greatest thing we can do in this world is not building bigger barns, it's not making higher salaries, it's not even becoming the most educated; the greatest things we can do is to love God with all our heart and with all our soul and with all our strength, and second to that is to love our neighbor as ourselves; starting with the one in the other room with the door closed - called your child.

Oneness

Dads, there is a spiritual uniqueness about the relationship of God the Father and Jesus Christ His only begotten Son. It is a relationship of oneness. I told you earlier about an event when my colleague and I were at a car museum and he asked the owner which car was his favorite and the owner of the cars asked him if he had children and he said that he did and the owner then asked him which of them was his favorite. Well, God has no favorites; the Bible says that God is not a respecter of persons, but God does have a unique relationship with His Son and the Son has a unique relationship with His children, that is, those who have accepted Him as their savior through His finished work on the cross. Dr. Lewis Sperry Chafer said, "No deeper revelation respecting relationship has been made than is set forth by these seven words, ('Ye in me, and I in you.')" KJV (John 14:20) He went on to say that the entire grace revelation is compressed into this twofold relationship. [13]

Dads, we, too, should not have favorites among our children, they are all a part of us, one is not better than the other, but they are all different. Unfortunately, we oftentimes give more glory and praise to the child who is more successful in life, however that is defined. I recently went to an event to hear Dr. Bernard Kinsey, who is an acclaimed collector of historical documents and African American artwork and artifacts; and is a world-renowned author. Kinsey was the first of two speakers and, like always, he really wowed the audience, and people were moved by his enthusiastic presentation.

The second presenter took the podium and said, "Wow" how do you follow that?" Then he began his presentation by telling a story about growing up with his brother, Harold. He told the story of how amazing Harold was as a kid growing up. He talked about how Harold was his hero and how even today, as grown men, Harold is still his hero. The second presenter was NFL Hall of Fame retired Oakland Raiders running back Marcus Allen. You see, dads, sometimes we look at what our kids do and have done and we put a value on them just like the world looks at very successful people and puts a value on their worth, but God looks at us like Marcus looked at his brother Harold, not for what he does, but for who he is. Dads, our love for our children is not based on what they become, it's based on who they are, our children.

| Reflections of
| our Image |

In the previous chapter I talked about us being created in the image of God as described in Genesis 1:26. However, there is yet another aspect to the image that I want to discuss in this section as it relates to the image of God. While mankind was created in God's image, according to the Scriptures, Jesus Christ is the "express image of His person..." KJV (Hebrews 1:3) The Apostle Paul described it this way in his letter to the Colossians: He is the image of the invisible God, the firstborn over all creation. For by him all things were created: things in heaven and on earth, visible and invisible whether thrones or powers or rulers or authorities; all things were created by him and for him. He is before all things, and in him all things hold together. And He is the head of the body, the church... NIV (Colossians 1:15-18)

When Jesus delivered his personal discourse on the subject of heaven, two of his disciples verbalized their questions and concerns. Thomas asked, "Lord, we don't know where you are going, so how can we know the way?" Jesus replied, "I am the way and the truth and the life. No one comes to the Father except through me. If you really knew me, you would know my Father as well..." Another disciple, Philip, said, "Lord, show us the Father and that will be enough for us." Jesus responded, "...Anyone who has seen me has seen the Father... Don't you believe that I am in the Father, and that the Father is in me?" NIV (John 14: 8-10)

Dads, these verses clearly describe the nature of the relationship that exists between God the Father and Jesus Christ His only begotten Son. Theologians call it a "Hypostatic Union." "The Hypostatic Union is defined as the union of two natures (dyo physes) of deity and humanity in the one hypostasis or person of Jesus Christ. It can be stated as follows: In the incarnation of the Son of God, a human nature was inseparably united forever with the divine nature in the one person of Jesus Christ, yet with the two natures remaining distinct, whole, and unchanged, without mixture or confusion so that the one person, Jesus Christ, is truly God and truly man."[14]

This union between Jesus Christ and God the Father presents for us a glimpse of what our relationship with our children could be except for the introduction of sin. Were it not for sin entering into the equation, we could share in an unbreakable union with our children. However, because of sin, there is a separation that occurs not only between us and God, but there is also a separation between us and our children. That is one of the reasons we are instructed to train up our children in the way they should go and when they are old they will not depart from it. Although our children are not "the express image" of us as Jesus is of God the Father, our children reflect what we instilled in them, whether through DNA or through training. Certainly, there are enough examples in Scripture where children did not reflect well the image of their parents. We can start with Cain, who murdered his brother Abel, and they were the first two sons born to mankind. There was nothing that Adam or Eve taught him that would make him kill his brother. But Cain became angry, according to the Scriptures, at God's response to his offering; even when God entered a dialog with Cain and asked him "Why are you angry?" "Why is your face downcast?" God even told him; "If you do what's right, will you not be accepted? But if you don't, then sin is crouching at your door; it (sin) desires to have you, but you must master it." NIV (Genesis 4:5-7) Many times our children are like Cain when it comes to sin; they have not learned to master it, thus, they do not reflect the image of parents who are further along in the process of learning to master their sin.

On the other hand, there are certainly plenty of examples in Scripture of children who did not reflect the image of their parents, yet they did what was right in the eyes of the Lord. I think of Josiah, who became king of Jerusalem after his father, King Amon, was assassinated. The Scripture says that King Amon did evil in the eyes of the Lord as his father Manasseh had done by worshiping idols. It says he forsook the Lord, the God of his fathers, and did not walk in his ways. Yet his son, Josiah, "he did what was right in the eyes the Lord and walked in all the ways of his father David, not turning aside to the right or the left." Dads, you have to know that your influence is generational. The Scripture could have said that Josiah walked in the ways of his great-grandfather King Hezekiah, but it goes back into his ancestry and pulled up King David who was the first righteous King of Israel. Dads, all I'm saying is that how we live and what we believe is reflected onto our children and it is the grace of God that causes them to follow our lead. And should they stray from the path that we taught them, it is the grace of God that causes them to return. Unfortunately, like in the case of Josiah, all too often our children are having to skip generations and call up ancestries to find the path.

My challenge to every dad who reads this book is to become the image that you want your children to reflect. One of the greatest compliments my wife and I have ever received is when people get to know our children and say things like "I know you came from good stock" or say Teresa and I did a good job raising them. I always have to remind myself that all we did was try to walk with God and follow His Word as closely as possible, which has been our recipe for parenting.

Humility

For most dads I would venture to say that this is one of the more difficult things to do— to humble ourselves before God and before our children. Dads are expected to know it all and have all the right answers. Sometimes our kids make us feel that way, but our wives quickly remind us that we neither know it all nor do we have all the right answers. In real life, unlike in television and movies, father doesn't always know best. As I grew up in the era of network television and saw the transition from black and white television to color TV, I can recall several shows in which the dad always had the right answers. There was even a show called "Father Knows Best" and there was "My Three Sons" and "The Andy Griffith Show"; then came "Good Times", "The Jeffersons" and "The Cosby Show." The common theme in these shows was that in nearly every episode at some point dad would get it right. On those rare occasions when dad got it wrong, he would eventually humble himself and apologize to his kids, and the stories would end with a loving embrace. That was television, but in real life it rarely goes that easily or that smoothly. You see, real life is more than 30 minutes with commercials; there are no commercial breaks in real life.

God the Father's relationship with Jesus Christ His Son embodies humility. It is not that God the Father was humbled, but rather that Jesus Christ, His only begotten Son, humbled Himself. So, dads, we learn our lessons in humility from the Son, not necessarily from the Father. How did Jesus demonstrate humility? Let me share five illustrations of Christ's humility:

1. **Humility – Jesus Meets the Woman at the Well**

   In the gospel of John 4:6-9, Jesus meets the women at the well and asks her for a drink of water. The woman, who happened to be a Samaritan, said to Jesus, "You are a Jew and I am a Samaritan woman. How can you ask me for a drink?" NIV (For Jews do not associate with Samaritans.) What this woman didn't know was that Jesus had predetermined their encounter; in verse 4 Jesus said, "Now he had to go through Samaria." NIV Jesus going through Samaria ensured that the gospel message of the kingdom would spread into Samaria. After discoursing with the woman, she said, "I know the Messiah (called Christ) is coming. When he comes, he will explain everything to us." Then Jesus declared, "I who speak to you am he." When His disciples arrived at the well, they asked Jesus why He was speaking with her. But the woman, having already been touched by her encounter with the

Savior, goes and tells everyone in town to "Come see a man who told me everything I ever did." The Bible says, "Many of the Samaritans from that town believed in him because of the woman's testimony: "He told me everything I ever did." And because of His words, many more became believers. They said, "We no longer believe just because of what you said; now we have heard for ourselves, and we know that this man really is the Savior of the world." NIV

Dads, when we humble ourselves like Jesus did and go where he went, God gives the increase. Sometimes we don't share the gospel with people because they are not like us, but God commended His love to us while we were all sinners. What makes us think that we are better than someone of another race, creed or religion? Regarding Jesus going into Samaria, the King James Version of the Bible reads, "And he must needs go through Samaria." KJV (John 4:4) Dads, where is it that you "must needs go through?" Wherever it is, humble yourself and go.

2. Humility – Jesus Wept

The second illustration is Jesus with his friend Lazarus. While the resurrection of Lazarus from the dead was one of the moments in the life of Christ where God the Father was glorified in the presence of many witnesses, it was also one of the extreme demonstrations of humility on the part of the Savior. According to the Scriptures, Jesus' friend Lazarus, whom He loved, had become sick and died. Upon receiving the news of his illness, Jesus declared that the sickness was for the glory of God that the Son of God might be glorified. (John 11:4) Four days later, Jesus arrived back in Judea and the Scripture says that when he arrived he learned that his friend Lazarus had died and had been in the tomb for four days. (John 11:17) Upon his arrival, Jesus is met by a grieving sister and many who came to mourn with her.

The sister of his friend said, "Lord, if you had been here, my brother would not have died." NIV (John11:21) What tremendous faith! Oftentimes this sister is thought of as not demonstrating as much faith as her sister Mary, who reportedly sat at the feet of Jesus while Martha worked and prepared the meal for their guest. But on this occasion, Martha demonstrated great faith in the power of Jesus Christ to have been able to prevent death and even in the resurrection at the last day. (John 11:24) Jesus turned her world around when He said, "I am the resurrection and the life. He who believes in me will live even though he dies. Do you believe this?" NIV Martha, at this point in the narrative, made another profound profession of faith when she said, "Yes, Lord,....I believe that you are the Christ, the Son of God, who was to come into the world." NIV

After professing her faith, Martha returned home and informed her sister that the one called the teacher (Jesus) had arrived and was asking for her. When they arrived where Jesus was, Mary did like she often did and fell at the Savior's feet. She, too, told our Lord, "If you had only been here, our brother would not have died." Like her sister Martha, she, too, believed in the power of God to prevent death. When Jesus saw and heard her and those who came with her weeping aloud, the Bible says that He was "deeply moved in spirit and troubled." This phrase demonstrates the humility of Jesus during their time of grief. It was his moment of compassion, but their moment of crisis, their brother Lazarus was dead. Jesus' compassion moved him to action and he asked, "Where have you laid him?" In other words, where is he buried? People often visit the grave site of loved ones long after they have passed on, but never in the history of mankind prior to this moment or since has anyone gone to a grave site to call someone back to life. However, Jesus was deeply moved and troubled in spirit and the Bible says that his emotions moved Him to weep. Oftentimes people, in their attempt to pray the shortest prayer they know over a meal, will say "Jesus wept;" yet they have no idea of the depth of what they are saying. "Jesus wept" is about God being in the flesh and dwelling among us. "Jesus wept" is about deity and humanity meeting at the crossroads called pain and suffering. "Jesus wept" is about seeing the glory of God. "Jesus wept" is about a man being humble enough to cry. I can rarely recall the times I saw men cry prior to coming to know the Lord. My first pastor, the late Bishop Odell McCollum, was one of the first men who I can recall would break down and weep during the preaching of the gospel. I suspect, like myself, when we think about how good God has been and how far He has brought us we become overwhelmed with emotions. This is one of the most humbling experiences that God has placed in my life. And as a dad who has the awesome responsibility of raising three kids to adulthood and Christian maturity, sometimes all I can do is to do what Jesus did.

Dads, Jesus lets us in on a secret if we will open our eyes and see it. Jesus said to Martha, "Did I not tell you that if you believed, you would see the glory of God?" You see, dads, most of the time we want to see, then we will believe; Jesus said, if you believe, then you will see. Our kids want to see us believe, then they will believe. Like I said, sometimes all I can do is what Jesus did. Notice in the narrative when Jesus had them roll the stone away from the tomb where Lazarus laid dead, Jesus prayed a prayer of thanksgiving in the presence of the people, for their sake. Jesus put God the Father's divine will and power in the spotlight that they might believe. Sometimes, dads, we have to put God's divine will, word and power in the spotlight so that our family might believe. I am reminded of Job when he had lost all that he had, including his health, and his wife said, "Job, why don't you just curse God and die." Job replied, "You are talking like a foolish woman. Shall we accept good from God, and not trouble." In all that happened to Job, the Bible says that he held on to his integrity and he did not sin in what he said. NIV (Job 2:9-10) Dads, we have to take a stand of faith on what God has said He would do. When Jesus prayed it was a prayer based on what God the Father had already said He would do.

The humility that Christ exhibited was contrary to that which is natural. By nature, we walk in the pride of life, we live our lives in and through the pride of our accomplishments. There is nothing wrong with being proud of your work or proud of your kids and their accomplishments, but more often than not that pride turns into selfish pride. It's like cholesterol, there is good cholesterol that we need to remain healthy and there is bad cholesterol which is harmful to our health. In Romans 12:3, the Apostle Paul reminds us not think more highly of ourselves than we ought, but rather to think of ourselves with sober judgment. The pride of life is one of three characterizations of the things of the world: "the lust of the flesh, the lust of the eyes, and the pride of life." All three are worldly characterizations and not from God the Father, according to the Scriptures. NKJV (1 John2:15)

3. Humility – He Girded Himself and Washed their Feet

Jesus provides us with many examples of humility, but one in particular I would draw your attention to is found in the gospel according to John 13. The example of Jesus washing the disciples' feet is one of my favorite biblical stories. The story is so rich with meaning that I would have to expand this book to do it justice. Christ came to do the will and work of his Father, and as the time drew near for him to depart and go back to be with his Father, he left his disciples with an indelible personal illustration and example of what they should be doing. The Scripture says, …Jesus, knowing that the Father had given all things into His hands, and that He had come from God and was going to God, rose from supper and laid aside His garments, took a towel and girded Himself. After that, He poured water into a basin and began to wash the disciples' feet, and to wipe them with the towel with which He was girded… Jesus went on to say,… If I then, your Lord and Teacher, have washed your feet, you also ought to wash one another's feet. For I have given you an example, that you should do as I have done to you.

There is so much wrapped up in these few verses, beginning with the analogy of Jesus rising from supper, putting on a towel and girding Himself and then the pouring of water into a basin.

Let me make these representations and, hopefully, you will see what I mean. Rising from supper – Jesus got up from glory in heaven and laid aside His garment. Jesus took off His glory that He had in heaven; John 17:5 says Jesus had eternal glory with the Father. He took up a towel and girded Himself – John 1:14-18 says He became flesh and we beheld Him as the only begotten of the Father. He poured water into a basin – Jesus shed His blood on the cross for the cleansing i.e. forgiveness of our sins; 2 Corinthians 5:21 and Hebrews 9:22 say that without shedding of blood there is no remission. With the same towel with which He was girded, He washed the disciples' feet – the towel represents His flesh. Jesus told His disciples, "If I do not wash you, you have no part with Me." Herein lies the richness, this was all done after supper ended. In ancient Middle Eastern custom, it was a common practice of hospitality to wash your guests' feet when they arrived at your home.

People often traveled great distances on foot through sand, rocks and dirt, and because they often wore sandals their feet would be dirty and needed to be washed, especially before eating a meal because they often sat low to the ground or on the ground with their feet exposed. The job of foot washing was normally assigned to a servant. If there was no servant in the home, then the woman of the house would wash her guests' feet. It was common practice in biblical times. Remember what Jesus said of Mary, that she washed His feet with her tears and dried them with her hair. In fact, Jesus rebuked Simon Peter by highlighting the fact that when He came into Peter's home, he gave Him no water for His feet, yet Mary did not stop washing His feet. (Luke 7:40-40) In 1 Samuel 25:41, the servant girl was called upon to wash the King's feet. In Jesus' day, widows who were provided for by the synagogue washed the feet of those who attended the synagogue as a means of earning their support. (1Timothy 5:10)

Foot washing was an act of cleansing that Jesus used to demonstrate the washing away of sin through forgiveness. The gospel writer of John makes an interesting observation as he concludes the record of this event. John writes: "So when He had washed their feet, taken His garments, and sat down again, He said to them,'Do you know what I have done to you?' Feet washing was normal, it was an everyday occurrence so what made this special, what made this different? This was different, this was special, and this was abnormal because this represented the glorious plan and work of God to bring about the forgiveness of sin. That is why Paul said in 2 Corinthians 5:19: "That is, that God was in Christ reconciling the world to Himself, not imputing their trespasses to them, and has committed to us the word of reconciliation." NKJV The end of this event represents the finished work of Christ on the cross when He said, "It is finished (tetelestai)." This signifies the completion of Jesus' work and the establishment of the basis for our faith. Jesus closed the event by saying to His disciples, "If you know these things, blessed are you if you do them." NKJV (John 13:17)

Dads, I didn't share this example of humility to rekindle the debate over foot washing and its relevance today; should we, should we not, that's not the issue. Although I have personally participated in a foot washing service and washed the feet of the church janitor, that's not the issue. The real issue is the lesson of humility that we learn from Jesus. Yes, He was the Teacher and, yes, He was and is greater than His disciples, but He treated them and loved them, and served them because they were not only His disciples, they were now His friends. These were the men and women who Jesus got to know in close human relations. Of course, He knows all of us intimately; in fact, the Scripture says that the hairs on our heads are numbered, but these, one might say, were in His inner circle. Dads, when it comes to our kids, they ought to be in our inner circle. They should observe and experience our humility like no other group of people; not the deacon board, not the ministers alliance, not your golf buddies, not your colleagues. No other group of people should be closer to you and have more observations of your humility than your wife and kids.

4. Humility – Gethsemane, the Olive Grove, a Place of Humble Submission

Matthew 26:36-46	Mark 14:32-42	Luke 22:39-46	John 18:1-11

We have looked at three illustrations of Jesus Christ and the humility He demonstrated before mankind. In the case of the woman at the well, He, being the Jewish Messiah, spoke with and brought salvation to the Samaritan woman, along with many other Samaritans. The case of Lazarus showed Jesus' humility as He wept for Lazarus in front of the people. In the case of the foot washing, He took the position reserved for the lowest servant in the house and washed the disciples' feet. Now Jesus makes a dramatic shift and His actions are before and toward God the Father.

Jesus had just finished the implementation of what we refer to in Christendom as "The Lord's Supper." It is where the clergy along with the congregation share communion together with unleavened bread or crackers and a small cup of wine; normally grape juice is substituted for the wine. In doing so, we remember the Lord's death until He returns, in obedience to Jesus' instructions to His disciples. As supper ended, Jesus described to His disciples the type of death He would suffer, and He let them know that His death would cause them to all be scattered. "I will strike the Shepherd, and the sheep of the flock will be scattered." NKJV (Matthew 26:31) Following these words, the synoptic gospel writers recorded the events that occurred in a place called Gethsemane; Luke called it the Mount of Olives; John said it was across the Kidron Valley and it was an olive grove.

When Jesus arrived in the garden of Gethsemane, the Scripture says that He had his disciples sit and keep watch while He went a distance away to pray. Dads, let me just stop here to say that sometimes we have to go off to a place of solitude and pray. Some situations call for a solo act between you and God; this was one of those times for the Lord Jesus. As a young man early in my Christian walk, while still living at home with my mother, I would go off to a small wooded area that led into Fairwood Park and find a large stone and sit there and pray or I would sit out on the roof of our house, particularly at night, and pray. These were my solo acts. Matthew and Luke picked up that Jesus prayed using the words "O My Father" and just "Father." However, Mark pointed out the term "Abba" Father. Now, we all have heard ministers and clergy pray using all types of introductory phrases: Heavenly Father, Dear God, Most Holy and Majestic God, Lord Jesus. Prayer introductions are pretty much what is on people's heart at the moment. I personally have a tendency to begin my public prayers with "Our God and our Father." For me, this puts God in the right place in the minds of the hearers. The One to whom I am praying is Our God, whom we worship, and secondly, He is our Father in heaven, the maker of all things in heaven and on earth. In my private personal prayers, I have a tendency to begin with an introductory phrase like "Father in Heaven." Again, in my own heart, it puts God in His proper place. It reminds me that I am not speaking to some guy on the block; I am speaking with my Father who is heaven. I am humbled to be in His presence.

The gospel writers tell us that this was an occasion when Jesus was deeply troubled and in anguish. Matthew and Mark both record that Jesus told the disciples prior to praying, "My soul is exceedingly sorrowful, even unto death." Luke records that Jesus was in anguish, and He prayed more earnestly, and his sweat was like drops of blood falling to the ground. It is in this context that Jesus prayed, according to Mark's account, "Abba Father." This double title that Mark recounts demonstrates for us the intimacy of the moment. Abba is an Aramaic word; Jesus often spoke in Aramaic. When Jesus would later ask, while hanging on the cross, "My God, My God, why hast Thou forsaken Me?" those words would be spoken in Aramaic; which lends itself to different interpretations than that of New Testament Greek. "Abba" was an intimate, more personal name in contrast to "Father," with which it is always joined in the New Testament. In the Gemara, which is a rabbinical commentary on the Mishna, the traditional teaching of the Jews, it is stated that slaves were forbidden to address the head of the family by the title.[15]According to Jewish tradition, Jews did not use "Abba" to address God because they perceived it to be disrespectful. However, because Jesus was and is the unique Son of God and on the most intimate of terms with God the Father, it was natural for Him to use the term "Abba," which essentially means "Daddy."

[16]When our kids use this term with us it, too, is a term of trust, familiarity and closeness that we call love. Jesus' familiarity and closeness with the Father and His trust in the Father enabled Him to pray: "O My Father, if it is possible, let this cup pass from Me; nevertheless, not as I will, but as You will....O My Father, if this cup cannot pass away from Me unless I drink it, Your will be done." NKJV (Matthew 26:39-42) Observe the confidence in Mark's account of Jesus' prayer: "Abba, Father, ***all things are possible unto thee***; take away this cup from Me; nevertheless not what I will but what Thou will. NKJV (Mark 14: 36)

Luke seems to bring out the calm assurance in his account of Jesus' prayer when he recounts it. "And he was withdrawn from them about a stone's throw, and kneeled down, and prayed, saying, 'Father, if you are willing, take this cup from me; yet not my will, but yours be done.'" NIV (Luke 22:42) Dads, what assurance we have to know that Jesus humbled himself in the face of His impending death with great confidence that the will of His Abba Father was greater, more important and more impactful than his own. Whatever we face as dads, we should always be willing to say as the Lord Jesus taught us to say, "Thy will be done."

5. **Humility – To the Point of Death on the Cross**

Gethsemane was a place of aloneness for Christ; even though He took his disciples into the garden with him, He went a stone's throw away to pray, only to return to find his disciples sleeping on three occasions. And when Judas betrayed him and the soldiers took him to be judged, all the disciples left him. Gethsemane prepared Jesus for Golgotha, which in the Aramaic language means the place of the Skull;

which is where they crucified the Lord of Glory the Lord Jesus Christ, the only begotten Son of God.

Being crucified was not only a hideous way to die, but it was a death of humiliation. Those who were crucified were often hung upside down and stripped of their clothes to enhance the shame. Their legs were broken to increase the pain and hasten what was a slow and painful death. The Scripture says, "Cursed is everyone who is hung on a tree." NIV (Galatians 3:13) But Jesus hung on the tree to redeem mankind from the curse of the law. At Gethsemane, Jesus prayed about the cup passing away from Him if possible, but nevertheless God's will be done; this is, that cup.

The Apostle Paul wrote to the Philippians Church in regard to Jesus Christ and said, "And being found in appearance as a man, he humbled himself and became obedient to death – even death on a cross! Therefore, God exalted him to the highest place and gave him a name that is above every name, that at the name of Jesus every knee should bow, in heaven and on earth and under the earth, and every tongue confess that Jesus Christ is Lord, to the glory of God the Father." NIV (Philippians 2:8-11)

In the discourse of the Good Shepherd in John 10:11, Jesus declared that He is the Good Shepherd, the Good Shepherd lays down his life for the sheep. In Israel and throughout that part of the world, in that day and time, the shepherds would call their sheep into the sheep gate or pen, which was walled by a two- to three- foot high wall, and the shepherd would lie across the entrance way all night to protect the sheep from thieves, robbers and wild animals. He would lay down his life for his sheep, not like someone who was hired, but like the owner he was; that is what Jesus did for us. Jesus went on to say, "I know my sheep and my sheep know me – just as the Father knows me and I know the Father – and I lay down my life for the sheep." Jesus added that there were sheep that He also had to bring. He said, "They, too, will listen to my voice, and there shall be one flock and one shepherd." He also said that this is why the Father loves him, because He laid down his life for his sheep. While the cross represented the murder of an innocent man on one hand, on the other hand, per Jesus' own testimony, "No one takes it from me, but I lay it down of my own accord." NIV (John 10:18)

Dads, the greatest love we can demonstrate is self-sacrifice that spares not life itself. Jesus said, "Greater love has no one than this that he lay down his life for his friends." NIV (John 15: 13) Our sacrifices begin at home with our families; our wives and our children must always come first in the order of priority when it comes to sacrifice. When I come home in the evenings, oftentimes dinner is on the stove, and I ask if everyone has eaten. The answer to that question lets me know how much I can eat. If someone has not eaten, then something has to be put aside.

Dads, I want to leave you with two final things as I close the chapter on this book. The first is that I hope and pray that as you have read this book, God has spoken to your heart and there are some things that you have identified in your own life that you are willing to change and to do better as it relates specifically to your children. Secondly, I leave you with the words of the Apostle Paul which represent where I believe I am in my parenting journey and what I believe we dads must do to practice faith-based parenting: "Not that I have already obtained all this, or have already been made perfect, but I press on to take hold of that for which Christ Jesus took hold of me. Brothers, I do not consider myself yet to have taken hold of it. But one thing I do: Forgetting what is behind and straining toward what is ahead, I press on toward the goal to win the prize for which God has called me heavenward in Christ Jesus." NIV (Philippians 3:12-14)

While this book has come to an end, my parenting journey has not. I will continue to support our three children and their dreams. My wife and I will continue to navigate the "uncharted waters" and we will continue to negotiate the "Danger Zones" that our children face every day. My commitment to our children and to you is that I will continue to learn from the biblical models and other godly fathers to become a better dad and to strive to be - "A man after God's own heart."

My hope is that young fathers will learn from my failures and my victories, along with the failures and successes of the biblical dads, and become better dads. My prayer is that men's groups will embrace the lessons learned to produce better dads. The hope is that fathers and grandfathers will take time to model good parenting before their children. My desire is that mothers would give this book to their sons, sisters would give it to their brothers, aunts would give it to their nephews, and grandmothers would give it to their grandsons so they, too, can become better dads.

SELECTED – REFERENCES

Berkhof, Louis. *Systematic theology*. New ed. Grand Rapids, Mich.: W.B. Eerdmans Pub. Co., 1996. Print.

Bright, John. *A history of Israel*. 3d ed. Philadelphia: Westminster Press, 1981. Print.

Burton, Ernest DeWitt. *Syntax of the moods and tenses in New Testament Greek*. 3d ed. Grand Rapids: Kregel, 1976. Print.

Buttrick, George Arthur. *The Interpreter's Bible (Vol 8) the Holy Scriptures in the King James and Revised standard versions with general articles and introduction, exegesis, exposition for each book of the Bible.*. New York: Abingdon Press, 1952. Print.

Chafer, Lewis Sperry. *Systematic Theology*. Dallas: Dallas Theological Seminary, 1948. Print.

Crockett, William Day. *A harmony of the books of Samuel, Kings and Chronicles: the books of the Kings of Judah and Israel*. Grand Rapids, Mich.: Baker Book House, 1951. Print.

Elwell, Walter A.. *Evangelical dictionary of theology*. Grand Rapids, Mich.: Baker Book House, 1984. Print.

Evans, Craig A., and W. Ward Gasque. *Luke*. Peabody, Mass.: Hendrickson Publishers, 1990. Print.

Evans, Tony. *Theology you can count on: experiencing what the Bible says about God the Father, God the Son, God the Holy Spirit, angels, salvation, the church, the Bible, the last things.* Chicago, IL: Moody Publishers, 2008. Print.

Gaebelein, Frank Ely. *The Expositor's Bible commentary: Matthew, Mark, Luke, with the New international version of the Holy Bible.* Grand Rapids: Zondervan Pub. House, 1984. Print.

Gaebelein, Frank Ely, and Richard P. Polcyn. *1 Kings - Job.* Grand Rapids, Mich.: Zondervan, 1988. Print.

Gaebelein, Frank Ely, J. D. Douglas, Dick Polcyn, R.D. Patterson, Willem A. VanGemeren, Allen P. Ross, J. Stafford Wright, and Dennis Kinlaw. *The Expositor's Bible commentary: with the New International version of the Holy Bible, Deuteronomy, Joshua, Judges, Ruth, 1 & 2 Samuel.* Grand Rapids: Zondervan Pub. House, 1992. Print.

Geisler, Norman L.. *Systematic theology: volume two: God, creation.* Minneapolis, Minn.: Bethany House, 2003. Print.

General articles on the Bible - General Articles on the Old Testament - The Book of Genesis - The Book of Exodus. New York: Abingdon Press, 1952. Print.

Gundry, Robert Horton. *Mark: a commentary on his apology for the cross.* Grand Rapids, Mich.: Eerdmans, 1993. Print.

Henry, Matthew. *Matthew Henry's commentary on the whole Bible.* New modern ed. Peabody, Mass.: Hendrickson Publishers, 2009. Print.

Hiebert, D. Edmond. *Mark, a portrait of the servant;.* Chicago: Moody Press, 1974. Print.

Hurtado, Larry W.. *New International Biblical Commentary—Mark.* Peabody, MA: Hendrickson Publishers, 1983. Print.

Joshua, Judges, Ruth, I & II Samuel: two volumes in one.. Reprinted. ed. Grand Rapids: William B. Eerdmans Publishing Company, 1985. Print.

Keil, Carl Friedrich, and Franz Delitzsch. *Commentary on the Old Testament in ten volumes.* 1971. Reprint. Grand Rapids, Mich.: William B. Eerdmans, 1982. Print.

Mackintosh, Charles Henry. *Genesis to Deuteronomy: notes on the Pentateuch.* [1st ed. Neptune, N.J.: Loizeaux Bros., 1972. Print.

Morris, Leon. *The Gospel according to St. Luke: an introduction and commentary.* Grand Rapids: Eerdmans, 1974. Print.

Murray, George Raymond. *Word biblical commentary.* 2nd ed. Nashville, Tenn.: Thomas Nelson, 1999. Print.

Radmacher, Earl D., Ronald Barclay Allen, and H. Wayne House. *The Nelson study Bible: New King James Version.* Nashville: T. Nelson Publishers, 1997. Print.

Ryrie, Charles Caldwell. *Ryrie study Bible: New International version.* Expanded ed. Chicago: Moody Press, 1994. Print.

Scofield, C. I., and Doris Rikkers. *The Scofield study Bible: New American Standard Bible.* Red letter ed., 1988 ed. New York: Oxford University Press, 1988. Print.

Tasker, R. V. G.. *The Tyndale New Testament commentaries.* Leicester: Inter-Varsity Press, 1974. Print.

The First and second books of Kings - The First and second books of Chronicles - The Book of Ezra - The book of Nehemiah - The Book of Esther - The Book of Job. New York: Abingdon Press, 1952. Print.

The Interpreter's Bible: the Holy Scriptures in the King James & Revised Standard Versions, with general articles & introductory exegesis, exposition for each book of the bible. In 12 vols.. Place of publication not identified: Abingdon Press, 1954. Print.

The Interpreter's Dictionary of the Bible Volume 2 E-J: an illustrated encyclopedia identifying and explaining all proper names and significant terms and subjects in the holy Scriptures, including the Apocrypha.. New York, N.Y.: Abingdon, 1962. Print.

Thompson, Frank Charles, and G. Frederick Owen. *The Thompson chain-reference Bible: containing Thompson's original and complete system of Bible study ....* 2nd improved ed. Indianapolis, Ind.: B.B. Kirkbride Bible Co., 1990. Print.

Unger, Merrill F.. *Unger's Commentary on the Old Testament.* Chicago: Moody Press, 1981. Print.

Vaughan, Curtis, and Virtus E. Gideon. *A Greek grammar of the New Testament: a workbook approach to intermediate grammar.* Nashville: Broadman Press, 1979. Print.

Vine, W. E.. *A comprehensive dictionary of the original Greek words with their precise meanings for English readers.* [Unabridged ed. McLean, Va.: MacDonald Pub. Co., 19. Print.

Walvoord, John F.. *The Bible Knowledge Commentary: an Expository of the Scriptures.* Wheaton, Ill.: Victor Books, 1985. Print.

Wood, Leon James. *A survey of Israel's history*. Grand Rapids: Zondervan Pub. House, 1970. Print.

Young, Robert, and R. K. Harrison. *Analytical concordance to the Bible on an entirely new plan: containing about 311,000 references, subdivided under the Hebrew and Greek originals, with the literal meaning and pronunciation of each; designed for the simplest reader of the English Bible*. 22d American ed. New York: Funk & Wagnalls, 19701973. Print.

MLA formatting by BibMe.org.

ENDNOTES

1   "George Gibbs, Blind Fight Trainer, Dies," Philadelphia Inquirer 1965: Print
2   Ibid.
3   Ibid.
4   Ryrie Study Bible, New International Version, Expanded ed., Chicago: Moody Publishers, 1994. Print
5   Glaze, Lauren E. "Correctional Population in the United States, 2010." U.S. Department of Justice Office of Justice Programs, Bureau of Justice Statistics, NCJ236319 (December 2011): 1-9. Print
6   Mackintosh, Charles H. Genesis to Deuteronomy, Notes on the Pentateuch. 1st ed. Neptune, New Jersey: Loizeaux Brothers, p.45 1972. Print
7   Ibid
8   Ryrie Study Bible. p13. Print
9   Unger, Merrill F. "Unger's Commentary on The Old Testament, vol. 1, Trans. E. A. Speiser. Moody Press, Chicago, p 63. 1981. Print
10 Morris, Leon. Tyndale New Testament Commentaries, 1st ed. Volume 3 The Gospel According to St. Luke, An Introduction and Commentary. Grand Rapids, Michigan: William B. Eerdmans Publishing Company, 1974. page 161. Print.
11 The Nelson Study Bible, New King James Version, Radmacher, Earl D. Th.D. Gen. ed., Ronald B. Allen, Th.D. O.T. ed., H. Wayne House, Th.D., J.D. N.T. ed., Nashville, TN., Thomas Nelson Publishing, 1997. Print
12 Buttrick, George Arthur, Commentary ed., "The Interpreter's Bible, The Holy Scriptures, In The King James and Revised Standard Versions with General Articles and Introduction, Exegesis, Exposition For Each Book of The Bible, In Twelve Volumes, vol. viii, Abingdon Press, Nashville, TN., pages 277-278, 1952. Print
13 Systematic Theology by Lewis Sperry Chafer, D.D., LITT.D., TH.D. volume 5 Christology, page 144; 1948.
14 Evangelical Dictionary of Theology, edited by Walter A. Elwell, Baker Books, Grand Rapids, Michigan, p 540. 1984. Print
15 Vine's Expository Dictionary of New Testament Words; Unabridged Edition; A Comprehensive Dictionary of the Original Greek Words

with their Precise Meanings for English Readers; MacDonald Publishing Company, Mclean, Virginia; W.E. Vine, M.A. page 11.

16 The Gospel of Mark; Walter W. Wessell, The Expositors Bible Commentary, Frank E. Gaebelein, General Editor, Zondervan Publishing House, Grand Rapids, Michigan; vol. 8 page 764.

ABOUT THE AUTHOR

George Gibbs - This first-time author has maintained a bi-vocational career for more than 30 years. He manages the Community Relations for UPS's West Region. George oversees the region's community affairs and philanthropic strategy. When not serving the community in his official capacity as the Community Affairs Manager, he serves the larger community as an ordained minister. He managed to find a way for the two disciplines to co-exist and harmonize in his life.

George earned his B.A. from Dallas Bible College, in Dallas, TX. He also earned a Certificate of Society for Human Resources Management (SHRM) from The University of Texas at Arlington. George also did graduate studies at Dallas Theological Seminary.

A native of Philadelphia, PA, he began his current career in 1980 in Dallas, TX, just weeks after starting college. He has held several positions of increased leadership responsibility in operations, business development, industrial engineering and human resources. Over the span of more than three decades, George has worked in numerous locations around the country, including several Texas locations and most recently Southern California. He simultaneously served in several leadership capacities within the local church. Most notably was his long term service on the Board of Elders at Bibleway Bible Church of Dallas, Texas.

He has volunteered his time and expertise to the community by serving on and working with several community and ecumenical boards and organizations, including: The Greater Dallas Urban League, National Urban League's Black Executive Exchange Program, The Orange County United Way Campaign Cabinet, OC Human Relations, Community Partners, Educate California and he currently serves as the Chairman of the UNCF Los Angeles Leadership Council. He is an Advisory Board Member of A New Day Foundation. He was recently elected to the Board of Directors for The Bernard & Shirley Kinsey Foundation for Arts & Education.

George and his wife, Teresa, have been married for 36 years. They have three young adult children: Courtney who resides on the East Coast, Tracey who resides in Southern California, and their son, Nathan, who currently plays professional basketball in Germany.

Printed in the United States
By Bookmasters